L11-74

L11-74

THE BOOK OF
WAISTCOATS

THE BOOK OF
WAISTCOATS

JACQUELINE FARRELL

With a foreword by Tom Gilbey

Create and customise
your own waistcoats
using embroidery,
fabric painting,
beadwork, appliqué
and a host of other
techniques.

THE
APPLE
PRESS

A QUARTO BOOK

Published by The Apple Press
6 Blundell Street
London N7 9BH

ISBN 1-85076-686-X

This book was designed and produced by
Quarto Publishing plc
The Old Brewery, 6 Blundell Street
London N7 9BH

Art editor Clare Baggaley
Designer Tanya Devonshire-Jones
Illustrator Jane Hughes
Photographer Laura Wickenden
Picture researcher Susannah Jayes
Senior editor Sally MacEachern
Editor Susan Baker
Art director Moira Clinch
Editorial director Sophie Collins

Typeset in Great Britain by
Central Southern Typesetters
Manufactured in Singapore by
Bright Arts Pte Ltd
Printed in Singapore by
Star Standard Industries (Pte) Ltd

CONTENTS

GALLERY
✱

TECHNIQUES AND PATTERNS
✱

PUBLISHER'S NOTE

As far as the methods and techniques mentioned in this book are concerned, all statements, information and advice given are believed to be true and accurate. However, neither the author, copyright holder, nor the publisher can accept any legal liability for errors or omissions.

BASIC SEWING EQUIPMENT
✱

For all the projects in this book you will need the following basic sewing equipment in addition to the items mentioned in the individual Materials lists:

✱

- Handsewing needles
- Pins
- Scissors
- Tape measure
- Thimble

A sewing machine is not essential, but will obviously be an asset, especially if it will do machine embroidery.

FOREWORD

I HAVE ALWAYS HAD A PASSIONATE BELIEF IN THE WAISTCOAT, A SIMPLE GARMENT THAT HAS SURVIVED FOUR CENTURIES OF FASHION CHANGES. DATING BACK TO THE 1580s, THE BASIC DESIGN HAS HARDLY ALTERED YET THE WAISTCOAT REMAINS A VERSATILE GARMENT, SUITABLE FOR ANY OCCASION.

TOM GILBEY

Evolving from its initial function as an undergarment, in the 1660s the waistcoat made a revolutionary British fashion statement. It became a reaction to the traditional doublet and hose as well as the flamboyant French fashions. The English diarist, Samuel Pepys, frequently referred to the new garment in his diary of 1660. Writing of the British King Charles II he said, "The King hath yesterday declared his resolution of setting a fashion for clothes which he will never alter. It will be a vest. I know not well how; but it is to teach the nobility thrift and will do good".

By contrast, Charles II's contemporary in France, Louis XIV, feeling snubbed by his action, initially relegated the waistcoat to the lower classes. However it was not long before he adopted it, dandifying the garment in the process by introducing richly embroidered fabrics and precious stones.

By 1825, Charles II's vision of the waistcoat reappeared again, being less "peacock" and more functional. It was not, however, until the latter part of the nineteenth century, when colour virtually disappeared from gent's wardrobes, that the more traditional woollen checks and plaids became popular. This was to coincide with the sobriety that was emerging as an integral characteristic of men's fashion. This theme lasted until the reaction to the austerity of post-war Britain, when in the late 1940s, men once again displayed their waistcoat plumage.

My own interest in the waistcoat goes back over 25 years, to when I first opened my couture house. I recognized that this simple garment served the purpose of a jacket but without the restriction that sleeves sometimes impose. Noting that it had been as much a favourite with the cowboys of the last century as with twentieth century rock guitarists – both requiring their arms to be unencumbered for easy access to the tools of their trade – I became excited with the idea of developing the waistcoat further, bringing it up to date to meet the needs of today's wearers, from office-bound professionals and dandies displaying their colours at night to outdoor activists such as bikers, cyclists, skaters, etc, who need uncluttered, dual purpose garments offering warmth and practicality.

JACQUELINE FARRELL

Today's modern manufacturing techniques, laser printing devices and performance fabrics allow the waistcoat to fit into any background as well as to suit all price brackets. Professionals, socialites, rock stars and labourers alike now have a means of expressing their individual style while still meeting the functional demands of their profession and pocket!

The waistcoat has a great past, a very varied personality and looks forward to a terrific and versatile future. Crossing all social boundaries, the waistcoat is to the '90s what the T-shirt was to the '60s.

Tom Gilbey

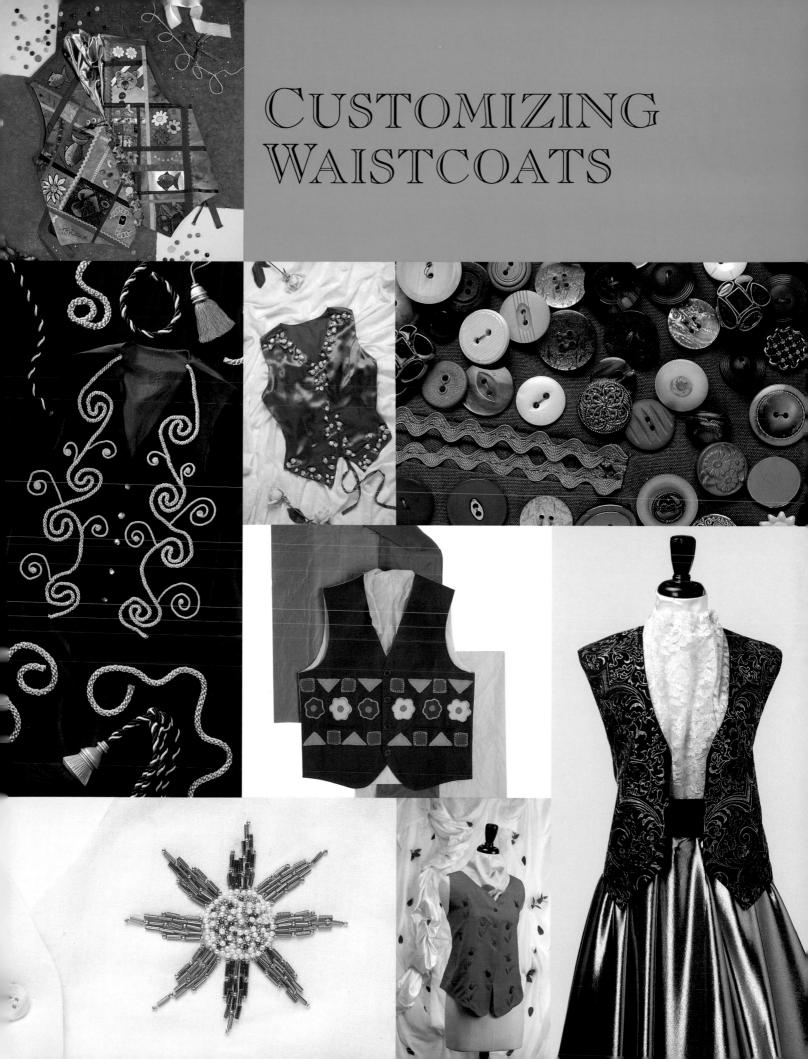

CUSTOMIZING WAISTCOATS

ROCOCO WAISTCOAT

THE CLASSICAL SCROLLS OF THE ROCOCO PERIOD IN DESIGN AND ARCHITECTURE ARE RECREATED ON THIS WAISTCOAT USING READY-MADE GOLD CORD IN TWO THICKNESSES TO GIVE ADDED TEXTURE.

✲ ✲ ✲ ✲ ✲ ✲ ✲ ✲ ✲ ✲ ✲ ✲ ✲ ✲ ✲ ✲ ✲

MATERIALS
✲

- Basic sewing equipment
- 2 m (2¼ yd) gold cord 6 mm (¼ in) thick
- 2 m (2¼ yd) gold cord 3 mm (⅛ in) thick
- Gold coloured sewing thread
- Sticky tape

✲ **TIP** *To create an interesting contrast the couching thread could be in a different colour or an unusual texture.*

1 Cut both the thick and thin cord in half and wrap sticky tape around the raw ends to prevent fraying. The thick cord will form the core of the design. The thin cord is used for the smaller scrolls.

2 Lay the waistcoat unbuttoned on a flat surface. Pin one sealed end of one length of the thick cord inside the right neckline. Pin the other end under the front peak, then lay the cord in swirls and waves down the front of the waistcoat. Experiment with the design at this stage. The cord will curl easily allowing manipulation. When you have a layout you are happy with, pin it in place.

3 Thread the needle with gold sewing thread and begin by oversewing the raw end of the thick cord underneath the lower edge of the waistcoat after carefully removing the sticky tape. Keep the stitches close together to form a "satin stitch" bar. This will secure the end and keep it looking neat.

4 The cord is "couched" onto the surface. Do this by stitching over and under it, through the waistcoat, keeping the stitches evenly spaced about 3 mm (⅛ in) apart. Continue up the front finishing at the neck with a "satin stitch" bar on the inside to cover the raw end.

5 Place the thin cord in scrolls at angles to the main line. Cut off about ⅙ of the length. Begin at the lower half of the waistcoat front. Gently push a raw end of the thin cord between the thick cord and the waistcoat. Pin it in place and sew a few stitches to secure it. Carefully trim off any excess cord that is showing through, then pin the length into a small scroll. Trim the excess cord and wrap all ends in sticky tape.

6 Couch the scroll in place, securing raw ends underneath the cord itself. Repeat small scrolls all the way up the front of the waistcoat varying the length of the cord and the tightness of the coil to create added interest. Repeat for the other side.

THIS FUN WAISTCOAT ALLOWS YOU TO RECYCLE NOT ONLY AN OLD WAISTCOAT BUT ALL

THOSE LOOSE BUTTONS THAT YOU KNEW YOU WOULD FIND A USE FOR SOMEDAY!

RAINBOW BUTTON WAISTCOAT

✿ * ✿ * ✿ * ✿ * ✿ * ✿ * ✿ * ✿ * ✿ * ✿ * ✿ * ✿ * ✿ * ✿ * ✿

MATERIALS
✿

- Basic sewing equipment
- Assorted buttons (approx. 300)
- 4 m (4½ yd) ricrac braid in a bright colour
- Strong button thread
- Sewing thread to match braid
- Tailor's chalk

1 Collect up all the loose buttons and lay them in groups according to colour: reds, greens, blues, pearly etc. You can either plan your button pattern in advance, or let it develop as you go along.

2 Lay the waistcoat unbuttoned on a flat surface. Using the tape measure and tailor's chalk, mark a line 2.5 cm (1 in) from all the edges on the front of the waistcoat.
  You can either remove the fastening buttons to apply the braid, then stitch them on top, or stitch the braid down alongside the buttons.

3 Cut the ricrac braid into 2 m. (2¼ yd) lengths. Begin by folding one raw end under and pin it to the front edge of the right shoulder seam 13 mm (½ in) in from the edge of the neckline. Pin the braid all the way round the right front panel, following the chalk line.

4 When you reach the buttonholes snip the braid and fold the ends through the top and bottom of the buttonholes. Pin it in place. The braid can be hand stitched using backstitch or machine stitched using straight or zigzag stitch. Trim the pockets if required.
  Finish off by tucking the raw end under at a side seam. Repeat for left side.

✿ **TIP** *Lighter weight plastic buttons without shanks are best for this project as they will lie flat, although you can use a mixture.*

5 Once the braid is in place you can begin to sew on the buttons. Thread the needle with the strong button thread and arrange a small group of buttons on the bottom left area of the waistcoat front. Sew on the buttons starting with the end of the thread securely knotted and finishing on the back by oversewing. Cover all of the left side of the waistcoat in this way.

6 Repeat step 5 for the right side. You could create a contrasting pattern by building up stripes of colour, or spell out a name, or initials to personalize your waistcoat.

✻ **TIP** *If the waistcoat front becomes very heavy you may need to sew light dressmaking weights into the back lining to prevent the front from drooping.*

VANILLA ROSEBUDS AND A DUSKY PINK SATIN WORK WELL TOGETHER ON THIS ROMANTIC-LOOKING WAISTCOAT. ALL YOU HAVE TO DO IS SOME HANDSEWING.

RIBBON ROSE WAISTCOAT

1 Divide the large and small roses into two equal groups, one for each side of the waistcoat. Lay the waistcoat on a flat surface and arrange the roses on it to experiment with the layout.

2 They have been randomly scattered around the border in this waistcoat, but a more formal design would work equally well. When you have achieved a design layout that you are happy with pin each bud in place.

3 Thread the needle and knot the end of the thread. Insert the needle from the back behind the rose nearest to the shoulder seam, preparatory to working down each front. Bring the needle through to the front then insert it through the base of the rosebud. Bring the needle down through the fabric to complete the stitch then repeat twice more to secure the rose.

MATERIALS

- Basic sewing equipment
- 36 (approx.) medium cream ribbon rosebuds
- 36 (approx.) small cream ribbon rosebuds
- Thread to match rosebuds

4 To continue, carry the thread across the reverse of the waistcoat and bring the needle up at the next rose. Stitch it in place.

5 If the roses are scattered widely begin and end each rose with a knot and oversewing. Do not carry the thread across large areas on the reverse as long threads may snag or break and will look unsightly.

6 Continue down each waistcoat front in turn until complete. For a truly delicate look you could sew rosebuds on instead of the existing buttons.

BOLD SHAPES AND COLOURS COMBINE TO MAKE THIS WAISTCOAT EQUALLY SUITABLE FOR
ADULTS OR CHILDREN. THE MAIN TECHNIQUE USED IS HAND EMBROIDERY.

EXOTIC EMBROIDERED WAISTCOAT

MATERIALS
✿

- Felt squares in the
  following colours:
  pink, purple, yellow,
  lime, green
- Stranded cotton: two
  skeins each of lime and
  turquoise
- Crewel needle No 4
- Scissors
- Felt tip pen
- A4 tracing paper
- 50 cm (20 in) square
  fusible bonding
- A4 light card
- Iron

1 Using the pen and tracing
paper, trace off one of each of
the templates below: square,
triangle, flower and centre. Trace
the shapes onto card and cut out.
Once trimmed, your card templates
are ready to use.

2 First lay the square on the paper
side of the fusible bonding
and trace around it eight times,
keeping the shapes close together to
save waste. Cut out the areas traced
and place them bond side down
onto the pink felt. Using a hot iron
bond them to the felt. Cut around
the shapes. Repeat for the
remainder of the shapes and
colours. Remove paper backing.

TEMPLATES

3 Lay the waistcoat on a flat surface. Place the felt motifs bond side down onto the waistcoat. Using a hot iron bond the motifs in place. The heat may take a while to penetrate through the felt so repeat as necessary but do not allow fabric to burn. A damp cloth placed over the design during pressing will help prevent burning.

4 Thread the needle with a cut length of 45 cm (18 in) of lime stranded cotton. Use all six strands. Begin either with a knot or catch the loose end under the reverse of the first few stitches. Start with a pink square and work the open buttonhole stitch (see Stitch Glossary). Finish by running the end under the reverse of the last few stitches. Use the lime thread around the pink squares and turquoise thread around the triangles.

5 Thread the needle with the lime thread. Begin as directed in step 4 but work a chain stitch around the outside edge of the purple flowers (see Stitch Glossary). Use the turquoise thread to work the chain stitch around the yellow flowers. The green centres are left unembroidered but will remain in place due to the fusible bonding. When the embroidery is complete, press lightly, using a dry cloth on the front and reverse of the waistcoat.

STENCILLING IS AN EXCITING AND EASY METHOD OF CUSTOMIZING A WAISTCOAT. THE COLOURS CAN BE AS SOFT OR AS INTENSE AS YOU WISH, AND THERE IS ENDLESS SCOPE FOR CREATING DIFFERENT DESIGNS.

TULIP STENCIL WAISTCOAT

MATERIALS
❈

- 3 medium-soft stencil brushes
- 1 fine soft paint brush
- Stencil paint – sunflower yellow, scarlet, pine green
- Kitchen towel
- Thin glazed white card or acetate A5 size
- Large sheet of medium-weight card
- Pencil
- Scalpel
- Tracing paper
- Masking tape
- Pins
- Glass jars

❈ **TIP** *If you make a* small *mistake with the paint, dabbing with masking tape may remove it.*

1 Stretch and pin one of the waistcoat fronts onto the card, making sure the fabric is quite taut. This will prevent it moving when stencilling.

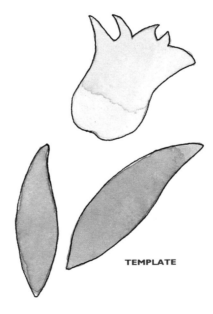

TEMPLATE

2 Trace off the stencil design onto tracing paper and rub it down onto white card. Carefully cut out the design using a scalpel.

3 Prepare stencil paint as directed by the manufacturer (each product is different). Creme paints were used here. Lay the tulip-head stencil on top of the waistcoat. Fix it in place with masking tape or stencil fixative. Dip a brush into the scarlet paint and dab it on a piece of kitchen towel to remove excess paint. Hold the brush perpendicular to the stencil and apply the paint in either a sweeping or circular motion, from the base of the tulip almost to the top. You can repeat the process if you want a deeper colour.

4 Dip a *clean* brush into the sunflower yellow paint and begin filling the stencil from the top of the flower head blending the colour as you go. Use the fine brush dipped in the yellow paint to add purer colour and highlights. This will complete the tulip head.

Remove the stencil, lay it on a sheet of kitchen towel and rub lightly with a clean piece of kitchen towel to remove excess paint.

5 Replace the stencil on the fabric and position the leaves. The stencil has been designed so that you can add leaves at various angles to make each flower totally individual. Tape or stick the stencil in place. Dip a clean brush into the pine green paint and fill each leaf shape with the green. Using the yellow stencil brush, stroke down from the point of each leaf to add lighter highlights. More detail can be applied using the fine brush with yellow paint.

6 The brushes and stencil can be cleaned with kitchen towel during stencilling, but should be cleaned after use with washing up liquid and warm water, or as directed by the manufacturer. For further information on stencilling see pp. 98–101.

GLITTERING BUGLE BEADS AND SEED PEARLS ADD GLAMOUR TO A PLAIN WHITE WAISTCOAT.

THE DESIGN WOULD BE EQUALLY EFFECTIVE ON A BLACK BACKGROUND.

BEADED SUNBURST WAISTCOAT

✺ ✺ ✺ ✺ ✺ ✺ ✺ ✺ ✺ ✺ ✺ ✺ ✺ ✺ ✺ ✺ ✺

TEMPLATES

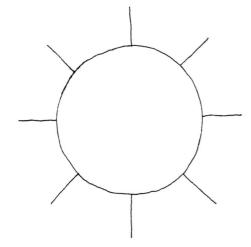

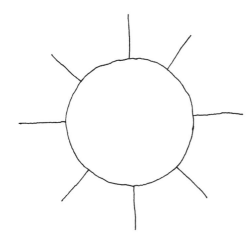

1 Trace off the templates (left) for each sun, then lay them on a light box or tape them to a window pane. Place the waistcoat on top and mark it with a water soluble pen. Alternatively, trace the circular shapes, trim around them, lay them on the waistcoat and mark round them with tailor's chalk.

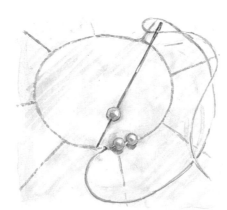

2 Thread a beading needle and knot the end of the thread. Bring the thread up from the reverse of the fabric to the front, at the edge of a small sun. Slide a seed pearl on the needle and insert the needle into the fabric. Use two stitches to secure the bead. Work around the circle edge attaching the seed pearls.

MATERIALS

✺

- Basic sewing equipment
- 1 packet of 6 mm (¼ in) gold bugle beads
- 1 packet of 2 mm (¹⁄₁₂ in) seed pearls
- 1 packet of 1.5 mm (¹⁄₁₆ in) circular beads in assorted colours
- Beading needles
- Strong fine white thread
- Air/water soluble pen, or tailor's chalk

BEADING LAYOUT

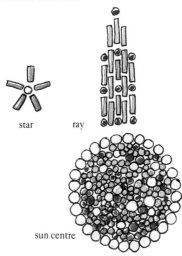

star   ray

sun centre

3 Stitch the sun centre with an assortment of seed pearls and circular beads, to create an interesting texture (left).

4 To make rays for the sun, follow the diagram (left) for your stitching. Remember to stitch each bead twice to secure it in place. Each sun should have eight rays about 4 cm (1½ in) long. Work the large sun in the same way as the small sun.

5 To make the stars, sew seed pearls on randomly, but evenly spaced, all over each front.

6 Surround each pearl with five bugle beads as shown in the diagram (left). You can make as many or as few stars as you wish. Fasten off and trim the threads after sewing each star. It is best not to carry the threads across the back of the waistcoat. For further information on beading see pp. 96–7.

ARTIFICIAL FUR PROVIDES A FUN ALTERNATIVE TO THE REAL THING AND IS EASY TO SEW.
USE OUR COLLAR PATTERN TO TRANSFORM A PLAIN WAISTCOAT INTO SOMETHING
MORE GLAMOROUS.

FUN FUR WAISTCOAT

❋   ❋   ❋   ❋   ❋   ❋   ❋   ❋   ❋   ❋   ❋   ❋   ❋   ❋   ❋   ❋

1 Trace off the collar pattern as directed in the techniques section on pp.114–15. Lay the fur fabric on a flat surface with the pile lying facing towards you. Fold the right sides together using just enough to lay the collar pattern on easily. Pin the pattern in place. Cut around the pattern through the fur. Repeat the process for the lining.

2 Pin the collar pieces right sides together, at the short edge. This should be marked on the pattern piece. Tack, then stitch them together on the machine using a straight stitch.

The stitches should be set at length 5 mm (³⁄₁₆ in) for this project to allow for the depth of the pile. (The tension will need to be adjusted as well. Refer to the machine handbook.)

Press open the seam with a medium iron and a dry pressing cloth.

Repeat all these stages with the lining, adjusting the stitch length and tension as necessary.

3 Pin, tack and stitch the fur collar to the lining, placing right sides together. Pin the outside edge of the collar all the way around; then tack and stitch. Trim off excess bulk from the seam allowance at the collar join, then snip small triangular areas from the edge seam allowance at regular intervals. Snip *close* to but *not on* stitching line. This will ensure the curved edge sits flat when turned right way out.

Turn the collar right side out, press and top stitch the seam about 5 mm (³⁄₁₆ in) from edge. This will also help the collar to sit flatter.

MATERIALS
❋

- Basic sewing equipment
- 50 cm (20 in) fur fabric (here, leopard print) 50 cm (20 in) wide
- 2 m (2¼ yd) cream bias binding (or background colour of waistcoat) 2 cm (¾ in) wide
- 50 cm (20 in) lining in cream (or background colour of your waistcoat) 114 cm (45 in) wide
- Cream (or matching) sewing thread
- 20 mm (¾ in) cover buttons (as required)
- Dressmaking shears
- Sewing machine
- Iron
- Pressing cloth (or clean tea towel)

❋ TIP *To avoid sewing mistakes practise on a scrap of fur fabric first, trying out different stitch lengths and tensions.*

4 Use bias binding to attach the collar to the waistcoat. Turn under 2 cm (¾ in) and press the raw end of the bias binding. Pin the edge of the binding to the raw edge of the collar through both fur layer and lining. Pin and tack all the way along the binding fold, then stitch the raw end under. Machine stitch in place.

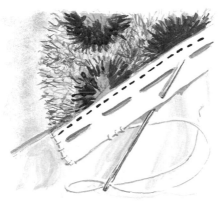

5 Pin the combined edge of the bias binding and collar to the inside edge of the waistcoat collar. Tack, then handsew them together. To hold the loose end of the binding catch it with a few hand stitches at the ends and at intervals along the inside.

6 To cover the buttons, trim circles of fur 5 mm (³⁄₁₆ in) larger than the cover button. Cover the button and fold excess fur to the inside, making sure there are no bumps or folds around the edge. Snap on the back plate of the button and sew it in place of a regular button.

THE SUMPTUOUS DECORATION ON THIS VELVET WAISTCOAT REQUIRES A STEADY HAND
AND SUBTLE COLOUR CHANGES TO ACHIEVE MAXIMUM EFFECT.

BAROQUE WAISTCOAT

❄   ❄   ❄   ❄   ❄   ❄   ❄   ❄   ❄   ❄   ❄   ❄   ❄   ❄   ❄   ❄   ❄

1 First choose your design. Bear in mind that it must work both as a repeat design and as a mirror image. You can enlarge or reduce your design on a photocopier to fit the size of the waistcoat or use the grid method shown on pp.118–9.

2 Place cardboard between the front and back of the waistcoat. To keep the waistcoat in place, stick it down firmly with masking tape. Transfer the design onto tracing paper with a chalk pencil. Place the tracing, chalk side down, on the waistcoat and fix it firmly in position with masking tape.

3 Using an HB pencil, carefully rub over the back of the tracing. It is very important to make sure that the tracing does not slip or the pattern will blur as it is transferred to the waistcoat. Check at intervals that the chalk is adhering to the velvet; you need a precise line for an ornate design. Gently remove the tracing paper.

MATERIALS
❄

- Tracing paper
- White chalk pencil
- HB pencil
- Masking tape
- Scissors
- Cardboard
- Liquid embroidery paints in bronze, silver and gold

4 Paint from top to bottom in one direction. You can either work on one area and then let it dry completely or move to a completely separate area where there will be no danger of smudging your previous work. For best results hold the nozzle slightly above the fabric and rest your wrist on a firm surface.

WITH IMAGINATION AND FLAIR YOU CAN COMPLETELY TRANSFORM A BOUGHT WAISTCOAT BY COVERING IT WITH RIBBONS, PATCHES AND AN ASSORTMENT OF FOUND OBJECTS RANGING FROM A CHILD'S TOY TO SHELLS. GREAT FUN TO MAKE, THE RESULT WILL BE ENTIRELY ORIGINAL IN APPEARANCE.

MAD, MAD WAISTCOAT

✣ ✣ ✣ ✣ ✣ ✣ ✣ ✣ ✣ ✣ ✣ ✣ ✣ ✣ ✣ ✣ ✣

MATERIALS
✣

- Basic sewing equipment
- Ruler
- Tailor's chalk
- Fabric patches – selection of colours and textures eg printed cotton, satin, lace, metallic cloth
- Ribbons – selection of different widths and colours
- Found objects, such as children's small toys, cracker gifts, shells, beads, bells or squeakers – anything that can be sewn or glued
- Glue
- Sewing machine (optional)

1 Use the ruler and chalk to mark a grid of diamonds or rectangles on the waistcoat. The chalk lines indicate where to sew the ribbon and also outline the areas for fabric patches or found objects.

2 Cut patches of fabric to fit neatly into some of the boxes or areas created by the grid. Pin the patches in place and try on the waistcoat to see the arrangement looks reasonably well balanced. You should also take the found objects into consideration (see Step 5).

3 When all the fabric patches have been pinned, sew on the ribbons either by hand or by machine. It is important to make sure that the ribbon is stitched to the waistcoat fabric and that it covers the raw edges of the fabric patches to keep them in place and to prevent them from fraying.

4 Turn the ends of the ribbon under at the edges of the waistcoat. Two sets of ribbons could be extended at the waist across the back to make a tie. A good way to finish off free ribbon ends is to roll and sew the edges and attach tiny rocaille beads to hide the seam.

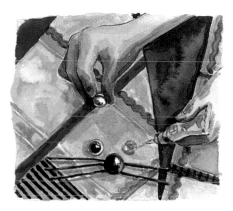

5 Arrange the found objects. Make sure that they are sewn or glued on firmly. Some items, such as the squeaker behind the teddy bear patch, may have to be put in position at an earlier stage. You can use anything you like to create a unique, personalized garment.

6 If the existing buttons are plain or dull, you could change them for something more exciting, such as these "smart" sweet-tube caps which are simply glued onto cover buttons.

THIS PROJECT IS QUICK AND EASY TO DO AND VERY FLEXIBLE. SIMPLY BY USING A PIECE OF FLORAL PRINTED FABRIC YOU CAN CREATE NUMEROUS DESIGN COMBINATIONS ON THE WAISTCOAT OF YOUR CHOICE.

FLORAL APPLIQUE WAISTCOAT

✽ ✽ ✽ ✽ ✽ ✽ ✽ ✽ ✽ ✽ ✽ ✽ ✽ ✽ ✽ ✽

MATERIALS
✽

- Basic sewing equipment
- 114 cm (45 in) wide floral printed fabric (approx. 1 m (39 in) depending on design and final application)
- 50 cm (20 in) fusible bonding
- Iron
- Pressing cloth

1 Choose the areas that you wish to use from your printed fabric. Points to note are: Is the design well defined? Are the proportions correct for the size of waistcoat? Can I get more than one image from the design ie; roses, buds, leaves, garlands?

2 Cut the fusible bonding into small pieces to match your chosen design areas. Lay them on the reverse of the fabric, bond side down and press with a medium iron on the paper side. Trim around each motif and the bonding. Continue until you have a selection of motifs.

3 Lay the waistcoat on a flat surface. Place the motifs on the waistcoat and experiment with proportions, arrangements and colour combinations. At this stage the design can be made as simple or as complicated as you choose.

4 When you have made your final selection, peel off the backing paper, lay each bonded motif back down and pin in position. When all the motifs are placed, press them with a medium hot iron and, if required, a damp pressing cloth.

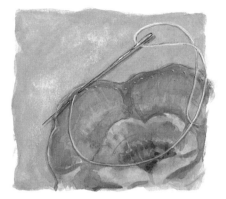

5 To ensure the motifs are permanent and can stand wear and tear it is best to stitch around each one using stab or prick stitch. Knot the thread and bring the needle up from the back. Then insert the needle just behind the point where it emerged, take it through to the back and bring it up again a short distance to the left of the first stitch.

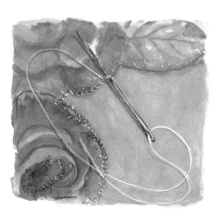

6 Make the next stitch as before and repeat the process around the motif. The result is a line of tiny dots around the edge of the motif and a neat line of stitches on the reverse. Finish by oversewing neatly. Repeat for all motifs.

MAKING
WAISTCOATS

THIS WAISTCOAT WAS INSPIRED BY THE COLOURS AND MOTIFS IN TRADITIONAL AMERICAN QUILTING. A CLASSIC RAW SILK FABRIC IN CREAM PROVIDES A PERFECT FOIL FOR THE RASPBERRY AND SCARLET HEARTS SURROUNDED BY DELICATE TENDRILS AND SAGE LEAVES.

SWEETHEART WAISTCOAT

❉ ❉ ❉ ❉ ❉ ❉ ❉ ❉ ❉ ❉ ❉ ❉ ❉ ❉ ❉ ❉ ❉

TEMPLATES

1 Cut up the fusible bonding into small pieces similar in size to the scraps of coloured fabric. Trace the outlines of the templates onto the paper backing of the bonding. Make as many of each shape as you need to decorate your waistcoat. Iron each piece of bonding to its corresponding scrap of fabric. Cut out each shape with small, sharp scissors.

❉ **TIP** *Before starting this project use some scrap material to try out the suggestions in the machine embroidery techniques section.*

MATERIALS
✿

- Basic sewing equipment
- 90 cm (36 in) raw silk (cream) 114 cm (45 in) wide
- 90 cm (36 in) fusible interfacing 114 cm (45 in) wide
- 152 cm (60 in) lining (cream) 114 cm (45 in) wide
- 45 cm (18 in) fusible bonding
- 5 × 20 mm (¾ in) cover buttons
- Rayon machine embroidery thread in jade and turquoise
- Tacking thread (dark)
- Sewing thread to match the lining
- Scraps of silk in raspberry, scarlet, sage
- Sewing machine
- Dressmaking scissors/shears
- Embroidery scissors
- Embroidery hoop (medium)
- Waistcoat pattern block
- Dark tailor's chalk

2 Lay the silk fabric right side up on a flat surface. Find the centre of the fabric by folding it in half, selvage to selvage, then mark it with pins.

3 Place the front waistcoat pattern piece right side up on the right side of the fabric, with the front opening edge lying along the centre of the fabric. Pin it in place. Mark the dart, then draw all around the edge with tailor's chalk. Reverse the pattern piece and repeat for the other half.

4 Tack around the chalk outlines. Using tailor's chalk, mark the seam allowances inside the outline. Your design should not go beyond these seam lines. Do *not* cut the panels out at this stage.

5 Peel the paper backing from the bonded shapes and lay them glue-side down onto each waistcoat panel. Fix them in place using a medium hot iron.

6 Using the embroidery designs (right) as a guide, draw embroidery guide lines onto the fabric using tailor's chalk. Try and vary the designs on adjacent hearts and leaves, and use scrolls of different sizes.

7 Start the embroidery by placing the bottom left corner of the panel in an embroidery hoop, making sure that the fabric is held taut. This will prevent the material from puckering when you are embroidering.

8 Thread up your sewing machine with the jade thread for the top thread, filling the bobbin with the turquoise thread. Set both the stitch width and stitch length to zero and detach the presser foot.

9 Slip the hoop under the needle arm and position it so that the fabric lies flat against the bed of the machine. *Lower* the presser foot lever to activate the tension spring.

10 With the presser foot removed there is no automatic feed, so the length of the stitches will depend on how heavily you press on the power pedal and how quickly you move the fabric. Start slowly at first, then gradually increase your speed, working in a continuous, fluid movement.

11 Move the hoop around the fabric to complete both waistcoat panels, making sure the fabric is always held taut. Remove the fabric from the machine from time to time to get an idea of how the overall design is developing.

12 Pull all trailing threads to the reverse of the fabric; knot and trim them. Press the fabric lightly on the wrong side to iron out any gathers. Cut out the panels and make up the waistcoat as described on pp. 108–11.

WITH A BASIC KNOWLEDGE OF KNITTING STITCHES YOU CAN CREATE THIS BRIGHT FUN WAISTCOAT WITH INDIVIDUAL FRINGING AND JAZZY BUTTONS.

SUNFLOWER KNIT WAISTCOAT

✿ ✿ ✿ ✿ ✿ ✿ ✿ ✿ ✿ ✿ ✿ ✿ ✿ ✿ ✿ ✿

Instructions are given for the first size, with larger size(s) given in square brackets [ ]. Where only one figure is given this applies to all sizes.

Tension

22 sts and 30 rows to 10 cm (stocking st) on 4 mm needles or size needed to achieve stated tension.

MATERIALS

✿

- Double knitting in sunflower yellow (see chart for quantity)
- Double knitting in lime and tangerine for tassels
- Seven fruit buttons
- 3¼ mm (No 10) knitting needles
- 4 mm (No 8) knitting needles
- Large tapestry needle
- Crochet hook
- Scissors

Measurements
To fit bust/chest

81	86	91	97	102	107	112	117	cm
32	34	36	38	40	42	44	46	in

Actual size

90	96	102	107	112	116	122	127	cm
35½	38	40	42	44	45½	48	50	in

Finished length

52	53	54	55	57	59	60	61	cm
20½	21	21¼	21½	22½	23	23½	24	in

Quantities
Double knitting

5	5	6	6	6	7	7	7	50 gram balls

Quantities of yarn are approximate as they are based on average requirements.

✿ **TIP** *It is important to check your tension before starting your garment. If there are too many stitches to 10 cm, your tension is tight and you should change to a larger size needle. If there are too few, your tension is loose and you should change to a smaller size needle.*

Abbreviations

alt=alternate; **beg**=beginning; **cm**=centimetres; **cont**=continue; **dec**=decrease by working 2 sts together; **foll**=following; **in**=inches; **inc**=increase by working into front and back of st; **K**=knit; **M1**=make a st by picking up horizontal loop lying before next st and working into back of it; **meas**=measures; **P**=purl; **patt**=pattern; **rem**=remain; **rep**=repeat; **RS**=right side; **stocking st**=1 row K, 1 row P; **st(s)**=stitch(es); **tog**=together.

Tw2R=K into front of second st on left needle, then K into front of first st and slip both sts off needle together.

Tw2L=K into back of second st on left needle, then K into front of first st and slip both sts off needle together.

Cr2R=K into front of second st on left needle, then P into front of first st, slipping both sts off needle together.

Cr2L=P into back of second st on left needle, then K into front of first st, slipping both sts off needle together.

Before starting to knit, read the instructions carefully and circle all figures relating to your size with a coloured pencil.

Cable panel patt (14 sts)
Row 1 – (RS), P3, Tw2L, P4, Tw2L, P3.
Row 2 and every alt row – K all K sts and P all P sts.
Row 3 – P3, K2, P4, K2, P3.
Row 5 – P3, Tw2L, P4, Tw2L, P3.
Row 7 – (P2, Tw2R, Tw2L) twice, P2.
Row 9 – P2, K3, Tw2L, Tw2R, K3, P2.
Row 11 – P2, Cr2L, K2, Tw2R, K2, Cr2R, P2.
Row 13 – P3, Cr2L, Tw2R, Tw2L, Cr2R, P3.
Row 15 – P4, Tw2L, K2, Tw2L, P4.
Row 17 – P3, (Tw2R, Tw2L) twice, P3.
Row 19 – P2, (Tw2R, K2) twice, Tw2L, P2.
Row 21 – P2, K3, Cr2R, Cr2L, K3, P2.
Row 23 – (P2, Cr2L, Cr2R) twice, P2.
Row 24 – K all K sts and P all P sts.
These 24 rows form cable panel patt.

Left front

With 3¼ mm needles, cast on 42 [**44**, 46, **50**, 52, **54**, 58, **62**] sts.
Rib row 1 – (RS), *K1, P1; rep from * to last 2 sts, K2.
Rib row 2 – *K1, P1; rep from * to end.
Rep these 2 rows for 7 cm, ending with row 1.
Inc row – Rib 1 [**2**, 2, **3**, 2, **3**, 2, **1**], *M1 (**by picking up horizontal loop lying before next st and working into back of it**), rib 10 [**8**, 7, **9**, 8, **8**, 11, **15**]; rep from * to last 1 [**2**, 2, **2**, 2, **3**, 1, **1**] sts, M1, rib to end. (47 [**50**, 53, **56**, 59, **61**, 64, **67**] sts).

Change to 4 mm needles and **patt, placing cable panel patt** thus:
Row 1 – (RS), K12 [**15**, 18, **21**, 24, **26**, 29, **32**], cable panel patt 14 sts as row 1, K48, cable panel patt 14 sts as row 1, K12 [**15**, 18, **21**, 24, **26**, 29, **32**].
Row 2 – P12 [**15**, 18, **21**, 24, **26**, 29, **32**], cable patt 14 sts as row 2, P48, cable patt 14 sts as row 2, P12 [**15**, 18, **21**, 24, **26**, 29, **32**].
These 2 rows **set** patt.

Cont in patt as set **working appropriate rows of panel patt** until left front meas 28 cm (or adjust to suit), ending with RS facing for next row.

Shape armhole and front slope
Next row – Cast off 3 sts, patt to end.
Work 1 row.

Next row – K2tog, patt to last 2 sts, K2tog.
Next row – Patt to last 2 sts, P2tog.
Next row – K2tog, patt to end.
Next row – Patt to last 2 sts, P2tog.

Dec 1 st as before at armhole edge on next and every foll alt row, **at the same time** dec 1 st as before at front edge on next and every foll 4th row until 34 [**33**, 34, **36**, 37, **38**, 41, **41**] sts rem, ending with RS facing for next row.

Dec 1 st as before at front edge **only** on every foll 4th row from previous dec until 23 [**22**, 23, **25**, 26, **27**, 29, **29**] sts rem.

Work straight until left front meas 52 [**53**, 54, **55**, 57, **59**, 60, **61**] cm, ending with RS facing. Cast off.

Right front

With 3¼ mm needles, cast on 42 [**44**, 46, **50**, 52, **54**, 58, **62**] sts.

Rib row 1 – (RS), K2, *P1, K1; rep from * to end.

Rib row 2 – *P1, K1; rep from * to end.

Rep these 2 rows for 7 cm, ending with row 1.

Inc row – Rib 1 [**2**, 2, **3**, 2, **3**, 2, **1**], *M1, rib 10 [**8**, 7, **9**, 8, **8**, 11, **15**]; rep from * to last 1[**2**, 2, **2**, 2, **3**, 1, **1**] sts, M1, rib to end. (47 [**50**, 53, **56**, 59, **61**, 64, **67**] sts).

Change to 4 mm needles and **patt, placing cable panel patt** thus:

Row 1 – (RS), K21, cable panel patt 14 sts as row 1, K12 [**15**, 18, **21**, 24, **26**, 29, **32**].

Row 2 – P12 [**15**, 18, **21**, 24, **26**, 29, **32**], cable panel patt 14 sts as row 2, P21.

These 2 rows **set** patt.

Work to match left front reversing shapings, working an extra row before armhole shaping and shoulder cast-off.

Back

With 3¼ mm needles, cast on 85 [**91**, 95, **103**, 107, **113**, 119, **125**] sts.

Rib row 1 – (RS), K1, *P1, K1; rep from * to end.

Rib row 2 – P1, *K1, P1; rep from * to end.

Rep these 2 rows for 7 cm, ending with row 1.

Inc row – Rib 8 [**4**, 8, **3**, 6, **8**, 4, **7**], *M1, rib 5 [**6**, 5, **7**, 6, **7**, 8, **8**]; rep from * to last 7 [**3**, 7, **2**, 5, **7**, 3, **6**] sts, M1, rib to end. (100 [**106**, 112, **118**, 124, **128**, 134, **140**] sts).

Change to 4 mm needles and **patt, placing cable panel patt** thus:

Row 1 – (RS), K12 [**15**, 18, **21**, 24, **26**, 29, **32**], cable panel patt 14 sts as row 1, K21.

Row 2 – P21, cable panel patt 14 sts as row 2, P12 [**15**, 18, **21**, 24, **26**, 29, **32**].

These 2 rows **set** patt.

Cont in patt as set **working appropriate rows of panel patt** until back matches fronts to start of armhole shaping, ending with RS facing **for** next row.

Shape armholes

Keeping patt correct, cast off 3 sts at beg of next 2 rows.

Dec 1 st at each end of next 5 rows, then on every alt row until 80 [**80**, 84, **88**, 92, **94**, 100, **102**] sts rem.

Work straight until back matches fronts to shoulder cast-off, ending with RS facing for next row.

Shape shoulders

Cast off 23 [**22**, 23, **25**, 26, **27**, 29, **29**] sts at beg of next 2 rows. Cast off rem 34 [**36**, 38, **38**, 40, **40**, 42, **44**] sts.

Make up

Omitting ribbing, press lightly following instructions on the ball band. Join shoulder seams.

Armhole borders

With RS facing and 3¼ mm needles, pick up and knit 135 [**143**, 147, **155**, 167, **171**, 179, **183**] sts evenly all round armhole edge.

Starting with row 2, work in rib as on back for 7 rows. Cast off in rib.

Border

With 3¼ mm needles, cast on 9 sts.

Row 1 – (RS), K2, (P1, K1) 3 times, K1.

Row 2 – K1, (P1, K1) 4 times.

Rep these 2 rows until border, when slightly stretched, fits up left front for woman/right front for man to start of front slope shaping, sewing in place as you go along.

Mark position of 7 buttons on border with pins to ensure even spacing, first to come 1 cm up from lower edge, last to come 1 cm below start of front slope shaping and remainder spaced evenly between. Cont in rib up left front slope for woman/right front slope for man, around back neck, down right front slope for woman/left front slope for man, then down to lower edge, with the addition of 7 buttonholes to correspond with pins on border, sewing in place as you go along. Cast off in rib.

To make a buttonhole:
(RS), rib 4 for woman/3 for man,
cast off 2, rib to end and back,
casting on 2 over those cast off.

Join side seams and armhole
borders.
Sew on buttons.

Fringing
To complete the waistcoat add the
tassels. Each tassel consists of 5
strands of yarn 15 cm long.
Alternative tassels can be made with
lime and orange yarn. The amount
required will vary depending on the
finished size of the waistcoat.

Begin the fringing on the right
front at the buttonhole band and
right front rib seam. Attach the
tassels using a crochet hook. Insert
the hook underneath the right front
and four rows up. Push the hook
through to right side, wrap five
strands over the hook and pull
through to underneath.

Draw loose ends over the front of
the waistcoat, then through the
loop, and tighten.

Place a tassel every second rib;
alternating colours, continue
around back and left front, finishing
at left front buttonhole band.
Repeat the process for the tassels
around the neck. Press and trim
ends even.

GOLDEN CHERUBS CARRYING HEARTS ALOFT DECORATE THIS SILK WAISTCOAT WHICH
WOULD BE APPROPRIATE FOR A WEDDING. THE CHERUBS ARE MACHINE EMBROIDERED.

CHERUB WEDDING WAISTCOAT

✷ ✷ ✷ ✷ ✷ ✷ ✷ ✷ ✷ ✷ ✷ ✷ ✷ ✷ ✷ ✷ ✷ ✷

1 Trace off the cherub template
(right) onto tracing paper.

2 Bond the gold dupion silk to the
fusible bonding with an iron.

4 Reverse the cherub template
and trace the cherub again on
the remaining fabric.

3 Lay the tracing on a light box or
tape it to a window. Place the
bonded silk paper-side down on top
and mark with a soluble pen.

5 Using the waistcoat template
given on pp.120–1, make a
paper pattern. Lay the pattern on
the cream dupion, pin and tack
around the edge. Mark darts.
Remove the pattern, then reverse
and repeat.

6 Cut roughly around each
cherub shape then trim it neatly
to within 1 mm (1/20 in) of the
outline.

7 Peel the paper backing off the
templates and lay each cherub
with the hearts facing to the centre.
The feet should begin about 10 cm
(4 in) up from the edge of each peak
and 4 cm (1½ in) in from the edge.
The bottom wing should be slightly
above the top dart marking. Press
each cherub in place.

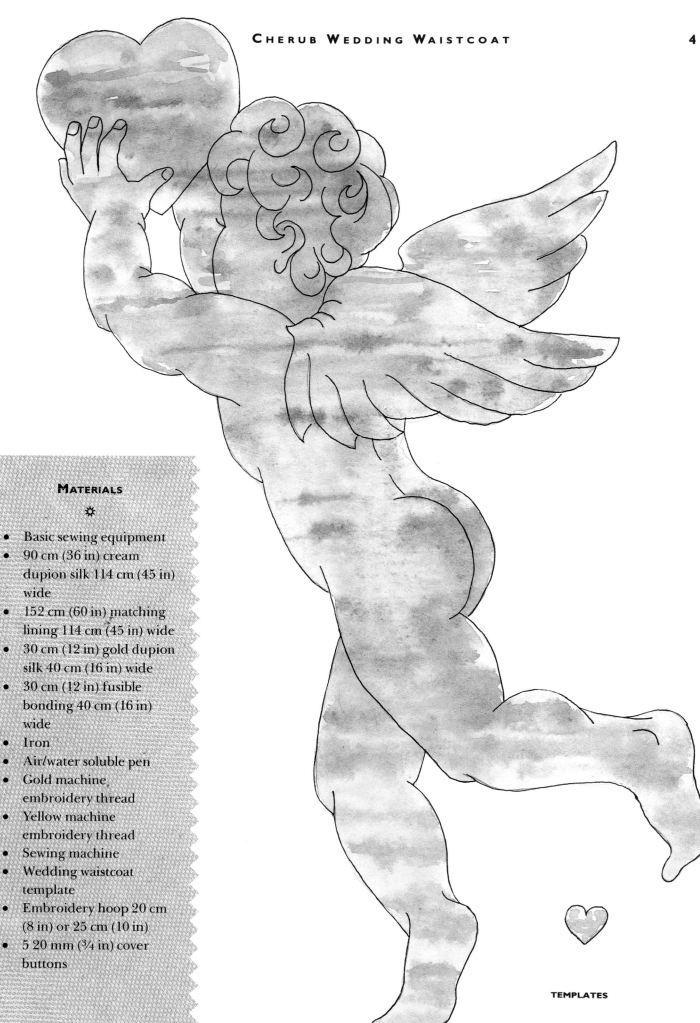

MATERIALS
☼

- Basic sewing equipment
- 90 cm (36 in) cream dupion silk 114 cm (45 in) wide
- 152 cm (60 in) matching lining 114 cm (45 in) wide
- 30 cm (12 in) gold dupion silk 40 cm (16 in) wide
- 30 cm (12 in) fusible bonding 40 cm (16 in) wide
- Iron
- Air/water soluble pen
- Gold machine embroidery thread
- Yellow machine embroidery thread
- Sewing machine
- Wedding waistcoat template
- Embroidery hoop 20 cm (8 in) or 25 cm (10 in)
- 5 20 mm (¾ in) cover buttons

TEMPLATES

8 Set up the machine to do free style embroidery according to the machine's handbook (or see pp. 94–5). The stitch length should should be zero, the stitch width zero, the presser foot removed and the feed dog down or covered with a darning plate. A darning foot can be used if required. The gold thread should be used as the top thread with the shuttle bobbin filled with yellow thread. *Lower* the presser foot bar to activate the tension. Practise first on a scrap of fabric stretched in a hoop. The stitches should be close together.

9 When you feel confident with your machine embroidery stitching, move on to the waistcoat. Stretch the design taut in the hoop and lower the needle to begin on a top wing. Stitch slowly and carefully around all the lines marked, going over lines twice, or even three times, to achieve a strong image.

10 Carry the threads across to different areas of the design when required. You can trim them afterwards as the thread should not unravel if the stitches are kept very close together.

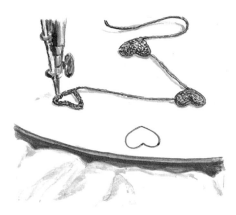

11 Using scraps of cream dupion, trace off the heart diagram and embroider it using the gold thread, filling the shape. Leave about 5cm (2 in) between each motif. You will find it helpful to use an embroidery frame.

12 Finish off by pressing the design with a damp cloth and a steam iron. Make up as directed on pp. 108–11.

13 Cover buttons by cutting out the heart motifs, making circles slightly larger than the button. Cover each button, keeping the motif central and snap on the back plate. Sew on the buttons.

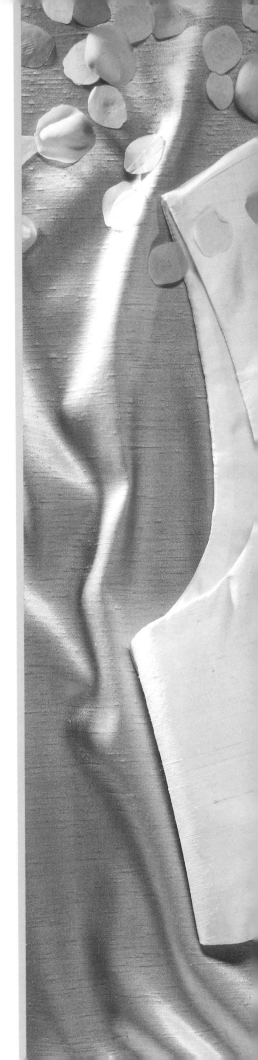

THIS WARM, COLOURFUL WAISTCOAT IS HAND EMBROIDERED USING BRIGHT TAPESTRY WOOL.
ONLY THREE DIFFERENT STITCHES ARE NEEDED TO CREATE THE DESIGN WHICH IS INSPIRED BY
TRADITIONAL MEXICAN EMBROIDERY.

MEXICAN FELT WAISTCOAT

✹ ✹ ✹ ✹ ✹ ✹ ✹ ✹ ✹ ✹ ✹ ✹ ✹ ✹ ✹ ✹ ✹ ✹

MATERIALS
✹

- Basic sewing equipment
- 70 cm (¾ yd) green wool felt 114 cm (45 in) wide
- Tapestry wool in orange, yellow, raspberry, jade (one skein of each) and scarlet (two skeins)
- Embroidery needle size 3 or 4
- Scissors (dressmaking and embroidery)
- Iron
- Tailor's chalk or bright tacking thread
- Green sewing thread
- Sewing machine (optional)

1 Trace off the pattern given for the Mexican felt waistcoat on pp.122–3. Lay the felt on a flat surface. Place the paper pattern, right side up, close to the lower right hand corner. (Do not place it exactly at the corner as each front panel will need a little extra fabric to enable it to fit easily into the embroidery hoop at the edge of the design.) Pin the pattern in place and mark the outline with tailor's chalk or tacking thread. Reverse the pattern piece and repeat for the other side.

2 Trim roughly around the two marked front panels to make this stiff fabric a more manageable size for embroidery.

3 Fold the remainder of the fabric in half and place the back pattern piece on the fold. Pin it in place, mark the outline with chalk and cut around the back panel. Lay it to one side.

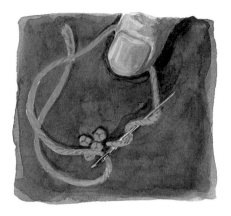

4 Mark the position of the first flower on each side by measuring 5 cm (2 in) up and 5 cm (2 in) from the inside corner of each front. Use tailor's chalk or a contrasting tacking stitch.

✿ **TIP** *For an alternative look, you could embroider the floral motif around the waistcoat edge only, or you could embroider simple leaf and stem shapes between the flowers.*

5 Now that the first flower centre has been established, mark the other flower centres which should all be approximately 8 cm (3 in) apart.

6 The flowers are worked in alternate colourways: jade and orange, then yellow and raspberry.
Thread the needle with the jade wool 45 cm (18 in) in length. Knot the end of the wool, or secure it under the first few stitches for a neater finish on the reverse. Bring the needle through to the surface at the first dot marked, hold the wool down using the left thumb and encircle the wool twice with the needle as shown.

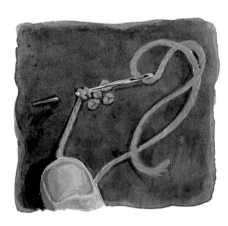

7 Continue to hold the wool taut while you twist the needle over and insert it close to where the wool first emerged. As you pull the wool through to the back the loops of wool around the needle will create a French knot.

8 Pass on to the position of the next stitch. Each flower centre has seven French knots. Secure the wool on the reverse by running the needle under a few stitches. Trim loose ends.

9 Use daisy stitch to work the petals. Thread a needle with the appropriate colour, secure the wool on the reverse and bring the needle up at the top of the cluster of French knots. Holding down the wool with your left thumb, insert the needle next to the point where the wool emerged, then bring the point out 1 cm (⅜ in) away.

10 Pass the point over the loop of wool and tighten it slightly to create a rounded petal shape. One tiny stitch over the end of the loop secures it. Repeat this around the central French knot cluster to form eight petals in total.

11 Once all motifs have been completed on each panel, cut out the pattern pieces. To join the fronts and back, stitch at the shoulder seams and sides using either straight stitch on a sewing machine or back-stitch if handsewing. Press open the seams. There is no need to overlock the seams as the felt should not fray.

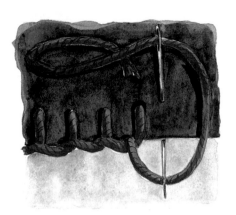

12 To give a decorative finish, oversew the edges in detached buttonhole stitch (blanket stitch) using the scarlet wool. Begin on the lower edge at one of the side seams. Bring the thread out on the lower edge, insert the needle again on the reverse at a position 1 cm (⅜ in) up, taking a straight downward stitch with the wool under the needle point. Pull the wool through the loop and repeat making the next stitch a short distance away.

13 The looped edge should follow the edge of the cut shape. Work around all the edges including armholes. Press to finish.

THE COLOURS OF THE SEA, SHELLS AND SAND COMBINE TO MAKE THE BACKGROUND FOR THIS
STUNNING CRAZY PATCHWORK WAISTCOAT. STARFISH, WAVES AND SHELL SHAPES FORM THE
BASIS OF THE MOTIFS.

SEASHORE PATCHWORK WAISTCOAT

❋ ❋ ❋ ❋ ❋ ❋ ❋ ❋ ❋ ❋ ❋ ❋ ❋ ❋ ❋ ❋ ❋

1 Enlarge the ladies' waistcoat pattern on pp.118–19. Scale up the templates noting which thread and pattern to use on each, following the key diagram (right).

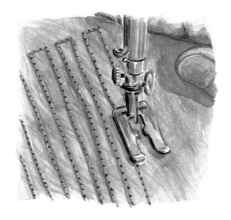

2 Lay out the antique gold silk and trace off the waistcoat fronts using either a fabric pen or chalk, or a running stitch. Mark darts clearly. Allow 5 cm (2 in) around the pattern. This will enable you to fit it securely into the embroidery hoop. Lay the paper templates for the areas marked 1 on top of the gold fabric and mark each area, according to the diagram.

3 To embroider, set machine for straight stitch using the coloured threads as directed on the diagram. The bottom tension should be set slightly looser than normal for all the embroidery in this project. Do this by slackening the small screw on the bobbin case very slightly. Practise on a scrap of fabric first. When the tension is correct the finished effect is of a main top thread dotted with "sparks" of colour from the bobbin. Remove the presser foot and *lower* the presser foot bar.
   Fill all areas marked 1 with straight lines 6 mm (¼ in) apart.

4 Mark out the template shapes for areas 2 onto the pink fabric. Leave an area of 5 cm (2 in) from outside edge to enable fabric to fit into the hoop.

5 Trace off the shell motifs onto the fabric using a vanishing fabric marker or chalk.

MATERIALS

☀

- Basic sewing equipment
- 1 m (39 in) antique gold dupion silk 120 cm (47 in) wide
- ½ m (18 in) bronzed pink dupion silk 120 cm (47 in) wide
- ½ m (18 in) glacier blue dupion silk 120 cm (47 in) wide
- ½ m (20 in) shot green (turquoise/gold) dupion silk 120 cm (47 in) wide
- 1.5 m (60 in) white silk lining 120 cm (47 in) wide
- 75 cm (30 in) fusible bonding
- Assorted reels of embroidery thread
- Embroidery hoop 20 or 25 cm (8 or 10 in)
- Scissors, dressmaking and embroidery
- Iron
- 5 × 20 mm (¾ in) cover buttons
- Sewing machine
- Buttonhole thread in white
- Tacking thread *or* tailor's chalk/fabric pen

MATERIALS GUIDE

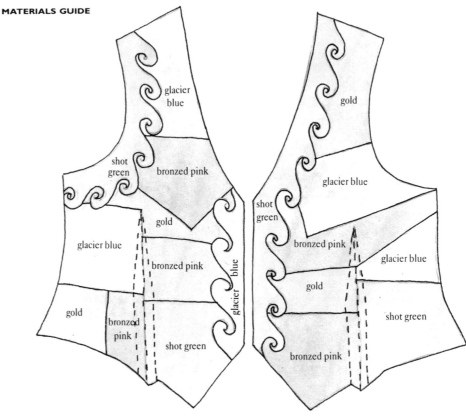

THREADS GUIDE

1 golden yellow top thread
   hot pink bottom thread

2 golden yellow top thread
   bronze bottom thread

3 turquoise top thread
   moss green bottom thread

4 tangerine top thread
   pale shell pink bottom thread

5 moss green top thread
   turquoise bottom thread
   (reverse for 5b)

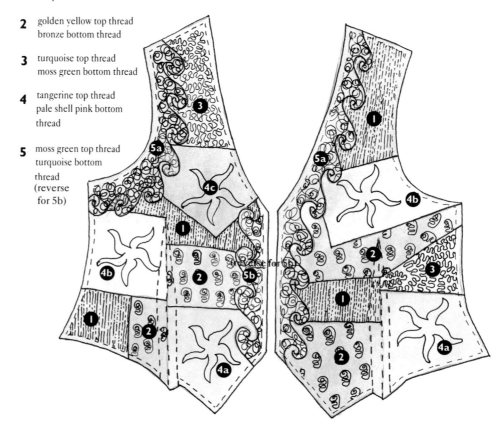

6 Always use a hoop as the finished result will be of a better quality. To do free embroidery, remove the presser foot from the machine and *lower* the feed dog. This will enable you to practise freestyle embroidery first, as directed in the techniques on pp.94–5. Thread the machine with the correct colours as shown on the diagram on p.49. *Lower* the presser foot bar. Start at the centre and spiral round 3 or 4 times then drop down 2.5 cm (1 in) before sewing a wavy line back to the top.

7 Mark out the templates on the blue fabric for areas 3 leaving a 5 cm (2 in) hoop allowance as before. Thread up according to the chart. Embroider the vermicelli pattern as shown on the diagram on p.49. There is no need to trace it off as the charm of this motif is its irregularity.

8 Mark out the templates for areas 4a, 4b and 4c, onto the appropriate fabric. Trace off the starfish design using a vanishing fabric pen.

9 Put the fabric into the hoop, set up the machine with the correct coloured threads and begin by outlining the starfish, then fill in with spirals of varying size and density.

10 Trim each embroidered panel, then iron them onto the fusible bonding and pin them in place before ironing them onto the gold base fabric.

11 Return all machine settings to straight stitch; ie attach the presser foot, raise the feed dog, reset the bobbin tension to normal and set the stitch length for 2 or 3. Sew around each patchwork piece using the correct toning thread; ie blue for glacier blue, bronze for bronzed pink etc.

12 Cut out templates for areas 5a and 5b – the "waves". Iron on the fusible bonding then pin and bond them in place as shown on the diagram on p.49. The fabric will now be quite stiff so you may not require a hoop. Reset the machine for free embroidery using the thread according to the chart and fill the waves with a continuous spiral.

13 You should now have two completed front waistcoat panels. Make up as directed on pp. 108–11.

14 Cover five buttons in the gold fabric embroidered with straight lines and sew onto the waistcoat front.

EDGE-STITCHED SCALLOPS AND A SIMPLE CUTWORK DETAIL MAKE THIS DELICATE WAISTCOAT

PERFECT TO WEAR WITH A SUMMER DRESS.

SUMMER WAISTCOAT

MATERIALS

❉

- Basic sewing equipment
- 142 cm (56 in) white cotton lawn 90 cm (36 in) wide
- White cotton sewing thread
- Scissors (embroidery and dressmaking)
- Sewing machine
- Iron
- Tailor's chalk or air/water soluble pen
- Stitch-and-tear interfacing 75 × 75 cm (30 × 30 in)
- 3.7 m (4 yd) white or contrasting bias binding (optional)

Cutwork motif with four distance marks. Use these to space your pattern correctly.

1 Using the cutwork waistcoat pattern on pp.122–3, trace off the front and pin onto fabric, mark around edge with tailor's chalk or pen. Reverse the front pattern and mark around it for the other front piece.

Fold the fabric and lay the back pattern piece against the fold. Pin and mark around it. Cut out the pieces.

2 Trace off the cutwork motif (left), onto tracing paper, including distance marks.

3 Lay the motif on a light box or tape it to a window. Place the waistcoat fabric over it beginning in the bottom right corner of the front right hand side. The motif should begin 2 cm (¾ in) from the seam allowance of 15 mm (⅝ in).

4 Trace the motif onto the fabric using the chalk or pen. Do not trace the distance marks.

5 Move the waistcoat along to trace each motif. For each new motif the distance mark should line up with the tip of the last petal drawn on the last motif. Each front should have six motifs.

6 Once the motifs have been traced onto the fabric, pin the interfacing in place on the reverse of the motifs. This will create a stiffer fabric on which to sew, and will overcome the problem of the fabric pulling or stretching.

7 To begin a motif, set the machine up with white cotton thread on top and bottom and set the control for zig-zag stitches. The shorter the stitch *length* set, the closer together each stitch will be, creating a satin stitch. (Practise on a scrap of fabric first.) Work around each petal shape finishing by leaving 5 cm (2 in) thread ends which should be pulled through to the reverse of the design, knotted and trimmed once all motifs have been stitched.

8 Using small sharp scissors trim away the centre of each motif very carefully.

9 Gently tear off the interfacing from the reverse of the fabric.

☀ **TIP** *To create a transparent effect repeat the motif at regular intervals all over the front panels.*

10 To make up the waistcoat set the machine for normal straight stitch. Pin the waistcoat wrong sides together at the shoulder seams and either side. Tack, then stitch these using a seam allowance of 15 mm (⅝ in). Press the seams open and oversew the raw edges using an evenly spaced zig-zag stitch to prevent fraying.

11 To finish this waistcoat, set the machine for scallop stitch if it has this control, otherwise mark a scallop detail around the edge using tailor's chalk and the template on p.52. Stitch over this line using satin stitch.

The scallop details should be worked 1 cm (⅜ in) away from the raw edge to prevent pulling. Trim away excess fabric. Press the finished waistcoat.

12 Alternatively, trim the edges with matching or contrasting bias binding all around the edge and the armholes.

THIS WONDERFUL DESIGN CAN BE CREATED USING FABRIC PAINT AND SALT! DETAIL IS ADDED
USING GOLD OUTLINER TO CREATE THE EFFECT OF LOOKING UNDERWATER.

AQUATIC WAISTCOAT

✹ ✹ ✹ ✹ ✹ ✹ ✹ ✹ ✹ ✹ ✹ ✹ ✹ ✹ ✹ ✹

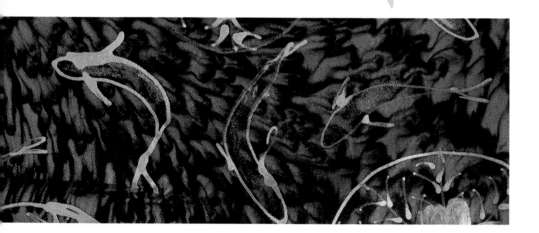

MATERIALS
✹

- 1 × 1 m (39 × 39 in) white silk twill (plus scraps for testing)
- 152 cm (60 in) black lining fabric 114 cm (45 in) wide
- Selection of paint brushes (very fine to 4 cm (1½ in))
- Table salt
- Iron
- Wooden stretcher frame 89 × 89 cm (35 × 35 in) approx.
- Drawing pins
- Deep green silk fabric paint
- Gold silk outliner pen

2 Cover your worksurface with newspaper to protect it and lay the frame on it fabric-side up.

1 Stretch the fabric onto the frame, holding it in place with drawing pins. Make sure it is taut, as it will stretch when wet with paint.

✹ TIP *If you have never done fabric painting before, test out the steps on scraps of fabric first.*

4 While the paint is still wet sprinkle small quantities of table salt over it. This will absorb and disperse the paint creating an unusual background effect.

3 Dip a large brush into the green paint and paint onto the silk in bold strokes, working fairly quickly. Do not worry about getting the paint even, as varied depths of colour will create a more interesting texture.

TEMPLATES

5 Leave the fabric to dry, then shake the salt off it. The length of time it takes to dry will depend on how wet you have made the fabric. Keep checking then remove the fabric from the frame.

6 Iron the fabric carefully using the "silk" setting, or a steam iron. The heat will "fix" the paint, but take care not to damage the silk.

10 Repeat the motifs at random all over the fabric until you achieve the desired effect. Leave it to dry. The gold paint is spirit based, so does not need heat to fix it. If you wish to iron the silk again, iron it on the back.

7 Re-stretch the fabric onto the frame, pinning it into position as before.

11 Remove the painted fabric from the frame and make it up into a waistcoat following the instructions on pp. 108–11. For further information on fabric painting see pp.98–101.

8 Begin to draw a design with the gold outliner pen (see Tip).

☀ **TIP** *If you do not feel confident about tackling the gold outline freehand try cutting card stencils traced from images in magazines or from the motifs shown. Even a simple circle repeated would work well against this textural background.*

9 Fish and abstract water lilies have been used here, but you could choose starfish, shells, seaweed or seahorses.

BRIGHT COLOURS AND DISTINCTIVE STAMP MOTIFS COMBINE TO MAKE THIS UNUSUAL STRIPED WAISTCOAT. SATIN STITCH EMBROIDERY IN GOLD HIGHLIGHTS EACH STRIP.

STARS AND STRIPES WAISTCOAT

❅ ❅ ❅ ❅ ❅ ❅ ❅ ❅ ❅ ❅ ❅ ❅ ❅ ❅ ❅ ❅ ❅

1 Make a waistcoat pattern as shown on pp.118–19. Fold the fabric in half and lay the waistcoat pattern at the open edge (not the fold). Trace the shape off and cut out the two front panels. Trace off and cut out the back panel and lay it aside.

2 Tape the fabric onto a flat surface, then mark the stripes. Begin 6 cm (2½ in) up from the point of the waistcoat, then lightly draw a horizontal line in pencil.

3 Continue to mark lines at the following intervals for both fronts: 1st 60 mm (2½ in) from front point; 2nd 25 mm (1 in); 3rd 100 mm (4 in); 4th 25 mm (1 in); 5th 75 mm (3 in); 6th 25 mm (1 in); 7th 100 mm (4 in); 8th 25 mm (1 in); 9th 75 mm (3 in); 10th 25 mm (1 in).

4 Use the large star stamp and the green ink pad to fill in areas A as shown on the diagram (right). Press the stamp lightly on the pad. Do not overload it with ink. Press it firmly onto the fabric but be careful not to move the stamp as this will smudge the image.

MATERIALS

❅

- Basic sewing equipment
- 70 cm (28 in) white cotton 90 cm (36 in) wide
- 152 cm (60 in) white silk or lining fabric 114 cm (45 in) wide
- Gold machine embroidery thread
- White sewing thread
- Ruler
- 2B pencil
- Sun/moon rubber stamp
- Large star rubber stamp
- Small star rubber stamp
- Fabric paint ink pad in green and purple
- Stencil cream (creme) paints in green, red and yellow
- Turpentine or paint thinner
- Selection of brushes
- Parcel tape or strong masking tape
- Five gold sun or star buttons
- Sewing machine

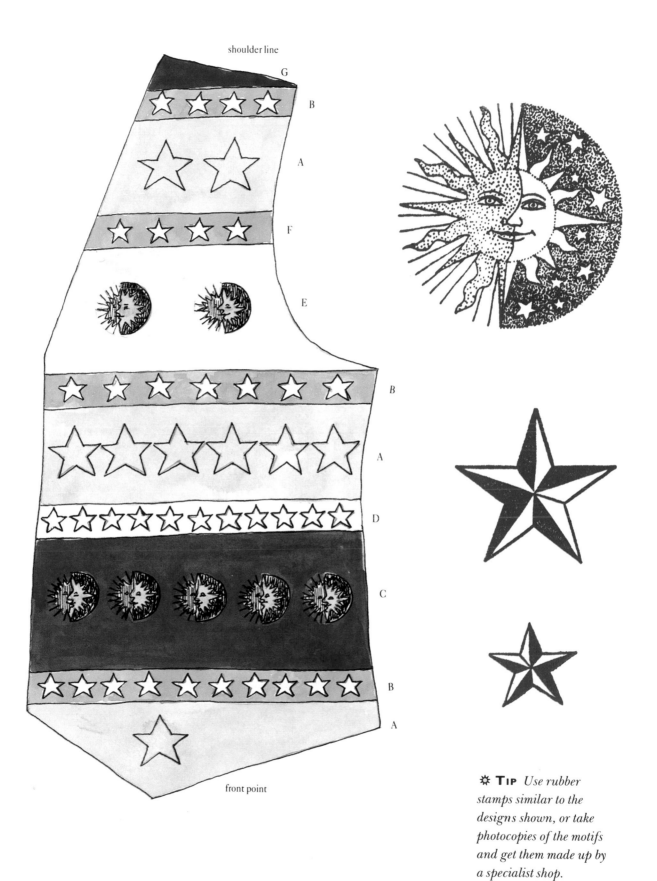

shoulder line

G

B

A

F

E

B

A

D

C

B

A

front point

☼ TIP *Use rubber stamps similar to the designs shown, or take photocopies of the motifs and get them made up by a specialist shop.*

5 Use the small star stamp and the purple ink pad and print areas B, D and F with the correct amount of stars.

6 Using the sun/moon stamp and the purple pad, print areas C and E with the correct amount of suns. Repeat for the other side. Leave the fabric to dry for a few hours.

7 Fill a shallow container with a little turpentine or paint thinner and use a 13 mm (½ in) brush with the yellow stencil paint. Wet the brush with turpentine then dip it into the paint. Do not allow the paint to become too runny. Cover areas A with the paint. You should be able to paint over the stamp motif without obscuring it.

8 Use a fine brush with the yellow stencil paint and fill in the sun and the rays leaving the moon-half white in area C and E. Fill in every second star with yellow in areas D and F.

9 Clean the brushes with the turpentine then use the red stencil paint to fill in area C; painting the area between the sun rays. Do *not* paint over the motif. Fill in area G with red.

10 Begin again with clean brushes and green paint and paint *around* the stars in areas B and F. Leave the fabric to dry overnight.

11 Set the sewing machine to do zig-zag stitch. Set the stitch length to very fine and the stitch width to the widest setting – about 6 mm (¼ in). Use gold thread for the top thread and the bobbin. Satin stitch along each line between the rows of patterns, covering the joins. Repeat for the other front.

12 Press the fabric with a medium hot iron to set the paint (see the manufacturer's instructions). Use a pressing cloth if required.

13 Make up the waistcoat as directed on pages 108–11.

14 To finish off the waistcoat, trim it with gold sun or star buttons.

✿ **TIP** *The stencil cream paint has been recommended because of its consistency as it does not "bleed" into other colours provided it is not thinned down too much.*

DELICATE ROSEBUDS ARE SCATTERED OVER A CREAM BACKGROUND. THE EMBROIDERY TECHNIQUE IS CROSS-STITCH ON EVENWEAVE LINEN, AND EACH MOTIF TAKES ONLY ABOUT AN HOUR TO COMPLETE.

ROSEBUD WAISTCOAT

�֎ �֎ ✖ ✖ ✖ ✖ ✖ ✖ ✖ ✖ ✖ ✖ ✖ ✖ ✖ ✖ ✖

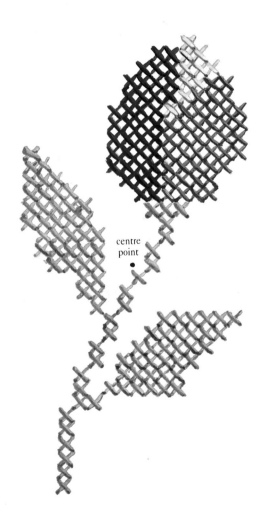

centre point

1 Trace off the waistcoat template from the patterns given on pp.118–19.

2 Lay the evenweave on a flat surface and pin the pattern piece in place, right side up on the right hand side of the fabric.

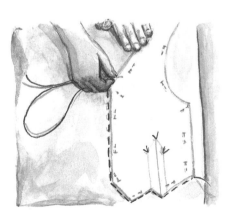

�֎ **TIP** *Cross-stitch can be worked from either the left or the right but it is important that the uppermost diagonal of all crosses should lie in the same direction.*

3 Tack around the outline and mark the darts.

MATERIALS

✾

- Basic sewing equipment
- Tapestry needle size 24
- 90 cm (36 in) cream even-weave linen (28 threads per 2.5 cm/1 inch) 90 cm (36 in) wide
- 152 cm (50 in) cream lining fabric 114 cm (45 in) wide
- Stranded cotton in the following shades: 1 skein each of pale rose pink, mid rose pink, deep rose pink; 2 skeins of lime
- Embroidery hoop 20 cm (8 in)
- 5 20 mm (¾ in) cover buttons

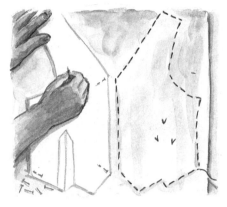

4 Remove the paper pattern and reverse it, then repeat the process. You will now have the waistcoat outline on your fabric.

5 Thread the tapestry needle with the lime embroidery thread, which is best cut into 45 cm (18 in) lengths. Use three strands.

6 To begin the first stitch, measure 6 cm (2½ in) up from the peak of the right hand waistcoat front. This point corresponds with the centre point of the coloured chart of the rosebud. Work the centre stitch first.

7 Do *not* tie a knot in the thread. Instead, leave a length of 4 cm (1½ in) on the back which should be oversewn by the first few stitches on the reverse to secure it. If this is difficult you can slip it under the back stitches later.

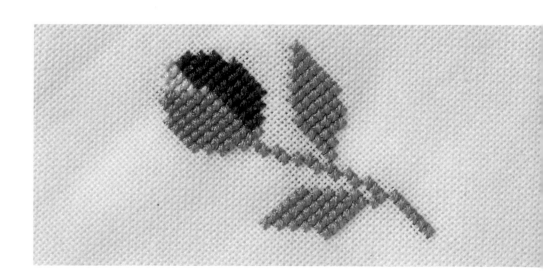

8 Bring the thread to the surface from the lower right hand side and re-insert the needle two threads up and two threads to the left and bring it out two threads down. You should now have a half cross. Continue this way to the end of a row if required.

✿ **TIP** *Stranded cotton usually comes in skeins of six strands. It can be used in varying thicknesses. For this project use three strands. To create a smoother thread it is best to separate all the strands then recombine the number you require.*

9 To complete a single stitch bring the thread from the bottom left two threads up and two threads to the right and re-insert. This will form the top half of your cross stitch. Complete all the crosses on the row.

10 Continue to work the stem and leaves in the lime thread before working on the bud.

11 Each bud has been placed 13 cm (5 in) from the centre stitch and alternate motifs have been reversed. Mirror and repeat the design for the left side.

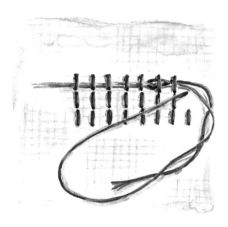

12 To fasten off the thread, run a thread under the reverse of a few stitches to secure it.

13 To complete, press lightly on the reverse and make-up as directed in the making-up section on pages 108–11.

14 Cover the buttons in a matching or a contrasting fabric as required and sew them on.

DEEP OCEAN BLUE VELVET HAS BEEN DECORATED WITH STYLIZED KISSING FISH. SPIRAL EMBROIDERY ADDS AN INTERESTING TEXTURE TO THE VELVET AND IS THE BASIC MOTIF IN THIS UNUSUAL DESIGN.

VELVET FISH WAISTCOAT

❋ ❋ ❋ ❋ ❋ ❋ ❋ ❋ ❋ ❋ ❋ ❋ ❋ ❋ ❋ ❋ ❋ ❋

DESIGN GUIDE

TEMPLATES

MATERIALS

✿

- Basic sewing equipment
- 1 m (39 in) blue velvet 114 cm (45 in) wide
- 20 cm (8 in) shot green silk 114 cm (45 in) wide
- 20 cm (8 in) shot gold silk 114 cm (45 in) wide
- 20 cm (8 in) shot pink silk 114 cm (45 in) wide
- 152 cm (60 in) black silk lining 114 cm (45 in) wide
- 50 cm (20 in) fusible bonding
- 1 m (39 in) lightweight fusible interfacing 114 cm (45 in) wide
- 5 × 20 mm (¾ in) cover buttons
- Scissors, dressmaking embroidery
- Embroidery thread in golden yellow, orange, turquoise, pink
- 40 cm (16 in) matching blue cord
- Embroidery hoop 25 cm (10 in)
- Sewing machine
- Iron
- A4 sheet of tracing paper
- Coloured pencil
- 2 sheets of A2 tissue paper

1 Trace off the pattern given for the velvet fish waistcoat on pp.124–5. Pin it in place on top of the blue velvet and tack around the pattern, marking all edges as well as the darts. Do not use chalk as it will mark the velvet.

2 Lay the fusible bonding glue side down over the heart motif shown and using a coloured pencil trace out six hearts, spacing them economically.

3 Trim the area with the motifs marked and iron onto the reverse of the pink fabric, glue side down. Trim around each heart.

4 Lay the tracing paper over the fish motifs A to D and trace using coloured pencil.

5 Reverse the paper. Lay the fusible interfacing glue side down on top and trace the motif A three times, spacing them economically.

6 Trim each section and iron them onto the reverse of the gold fabric. Trim around each fish.

7 Repeat motif A, tracing it onto the fusible bonding four times. Trim and iron these on the reverse of the green fabric (the fourth motif is worked around the dart marking). Trim around the fish.

8 Repeat for motif B – 3 × gold, 4 × green; motif C – 3 × gold, 3 × green; motif D – 3 × gold, 3 × green. You should now have 26 fish and 6 hearts trimmed and ready to be placed onto the waistcoat.

9 Following the diagram (left) enlarge to full size and trace the outlines. Pin onto velvet, then tack the outline edge of the design. Mark the centre points of the hearts. Pin the hearts and kissing fish in place.

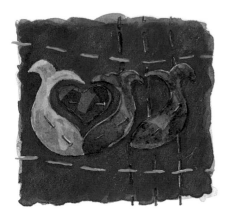

10 Add in the extra dart fish and single fish. Press them in place.

11 Set the machine to do free embroidery by removing the presser foot and lowering the feed dog. Thread the machine with turquoise top thread and pink bobbin thread. Loosen the bobbin thread tension slightly by turning the screw on the bobbin case. This will create a series of small dots of pink on top of the turquoise thread during embroidery.

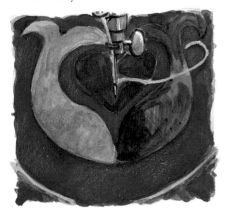

12 Insert the fabric into the hoop. Place this on the machine and *lower* the presser foot bar to activate the tension. Begin to embroider around the outline of each fish slowly but smoothly following the diagram on p.68.

13 Make a line for the fish head about 1 cm (⅜ in) from the tip then make a spiral for the eye before filling the body part with "scales". Repeat for all the fish, then outline each heart.

14 Thread the machine with an orange top thread and a yellow bobbin thread. Mark with tacking stitches, areas to be given swirls. Work within the shapes you have tacked and fill them with swirls. Do not outline them unless you want a more solid effect.

15 Link each fish motif with a simple wavy line embellished with two swirls. Remove tacking stitches.

16 Trim each panel and make up as directed on pp. 108–11. Cut the blue cord into five even lengths and stitch one to the left side of the waistcoat on top of the lining. Wrap each stitch over the cord loop until you have a smooth band of satin stitching. This will prevent fraying. Repeat for other four loops. Cover five buttons in velvet embroidered with gold swirls as before and stitch them in place down the right hand side of the waistcoat as shown on p.68.

MIXED MEDIA

This striking collection shows what an ideal garment the waistcoat is for demonstrating a variety of decorative techniques. Some techniques are combined to create more intricate effects, for example screen-printed fabric can be worked into patchwork designs before being embroidered.

CAROLINE KEILL
(above and right)
Screen-printed velvet has been embossed using couched gold thread and machine embroidery. The back panel is made from a recycled curtain.

TORIA CHAUMETON
(top and bottom)
A vivid palette of mixed shades of crushed velvet and silk are patched in squares alongside randomly placed printed patches in coordinating colours.

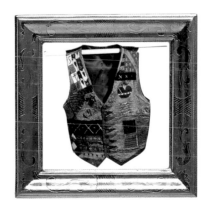

CAROLINE KEILL
(above)
Screen-printed gold and black
fabrics have been patched
together in strips and
highlighted by embroidering
with metallic threads.

ROSEMARY MacCARTHY-
MORROGH *(top)*
A photograph of a cluster of
daisies was the inspiration for
this waistcoat, which was worked
on white linen, hand-painted,
embroidered and beaded.

DEBORAH GONET
(bottom)
The traditional colours and
shapes of heraldic symbols are
recreated using a combination of
machine embroidery and
patched silk and velvet.

MACHINE
EMBROIDERY AND APPLIQUÉ

Jacqueline Farrell's waistcoats are mainly
created from luxury fabrics such as linen
and silk. Her favourite technique is machine
embroidery over appliqué shapes with
imagery derived from natural forms and
contemporary motifs.

JACQUELINE FARRELL
(above left)
Bright bluebells, rosebuds and
others are appliquéd on dupion
and attached by free machine
embroidery.

JACQUELINE FARRELL
(above centre)
A bold design on linen-look silk
is given a delicate touch with
machine embroidery.

JACQUELINE FARRELL
(above right)
Appliquéd stars in bright
colours and whimsical detail in
bright green thread give a
lighthearted, festive impression.

JACQUELINE FARRELL
(above left)
Rambling ivy leaves entwined
with little purple flowers are
appliquéd onto velvet, quilted
with machine embroidery.

JACQUELINE FARRELL
(above centre)
Bold sunflowers appliquéd onto
silk dupion are interlaced with
machine-embroidered scrolls
and a scattering of leaves.

JACQUELINE FARRELL
(above right)
Black velvet provides the foil for
the crimson roses creating a
winter colour scheme. The detail
is machine embroidery.

WOVEN AND PATCHWORK WAISTCOATS

Hand-woven fabrics can create lovely textural waistcoats which can either exploit the fabric texture or focus on the colour. An effective way of employing colour is to use one colour in a variety of shades in a patchwork combination.

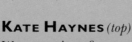

KATE HAYNES *(top)*
Woven stripes form a cotton and silk doublecloth fabric. *(centre)* The weave technique of "figuring" allows distinct images to be created at strategic points.

POOKIE BLEZARD
(right)
Earthy tones, well-balanced proportions and interesting textures combine successfully in this patchwork waistcoat.

GEORGINA VON ETZDORF
(opposite left)
Gold and wine corded fabric gives this woven fabric waistcoat a warm, rich look.

KATE HAYNES
(top centre)
Minimalist colour and hand-woven pleats produce a wonderfully understated waistcoat in cool tones.

JANET GEORGE *(bottom)*
An intricately woven wool fabric in bright variegated bands and a rich red tartan are made into two waistcoats with classic lines.

TORIA CHAUMETON
(top right)
Harlequin checked silk in heraldic colours makes a stylish waistcoat. Note the neat collar revers.

APPLIQUÉ AND PATCHWORK

Patchwork is an economic and effective method of using up small pieces of fabric. To add extra detail, the patchwork fabric can be quilted or embroidered after construction.

DEBORAH GONET

(bottom)

Individual squares of silks and velvets are appliquéd and embroidered with a kaleidescope of images and textures.

JUDITH GAIT

(top right)

Crazy patchwork using silk dupion fabric in three colours is overstitched with contrasting machine embroidery in satin stitch.

POOKIE BLEZARD

(bottom)

Two waistcoat shapes and one technique: patchwork strips. A high stand-up collar offers an alternative to the traditional V-neck waistcoat.

✼ ✼ ✼ ✼ ✼ ✼ ✼ ✼ ✼ ✼ ✼ ✼ ✼ ✼ ✼ ✼

DEBORAH GONET

(top)

Huge fun sunflowers are appliquéd onto this plain linen waistcoat. The edges are left raw and deliberately frayed for a realistic look which adds texture.

TORIA CHAUMETON

(far top left)

Toning strips of tapestry fabrics are stitched together to produce a unique patchwork fabric for this handsome waistcoat. *(above right and centre)* This magnificent long-line waistcoat in stained-glass patchwork features a wonderful array of floral prints.

TAILORED WAISTCOATS

Tailored waistcoats require more complex techniques than the making-up featured in this book. However, Tom Gilbey's creative use of sumptuous materials, hand-painting, screen-printing, embroidery and other details provides great inspiration.

TOM GILBEY

(above left)

This bold heraldic imagery is created from machine embroidered appliqué, decorated with sparkling jewels.

TOM GILBEY

(above centre)

Black and white images of famous people and places are screen printed onto white silk, so that the overall design is graded from dark to light.

TOM GILBEY

(above right)

Fun metal and fabric badges with images based on a transport theme customize a bought waistcoat. This is a great way of using souvenirs.

TOM GILBEY
(above top and bottom)
This exclusive image from an auctioneers' showroom lends itself to being hand-painted onto silk in subtle tones which are carried through to the back.

TOM GILBEY
(above centre)
Quilted hearts interlaced with gold embroidery and three-dimensional gold roses stand out on a cream silk background.

TOM GILBEY
(above right)
A glossy black background fabric is the perfect foil for pretty floral tapestry hearts. The appliquéd hearts are interlinked with couched gold cord.

APPLIQUÉ AND EMBROIDERY

Any material can be used to decorate waistcoats, as this collection shows. Appliquéd strips of ribbon are effective and distorted handknitting creates an unusual fabric texture. Both ideas and materials can be "recycled" in this way.

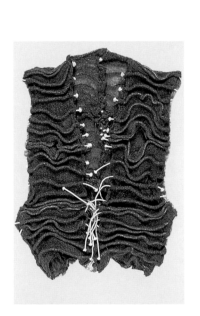

JANET AND ROGER QUILTER
(left and centre)
Appliqué images, based on characters from Dylan Thomas' Under Milkwood, are quilted onto this pictorial waistcoat.

JO HALL
(bottom right)
This fragile-looking waistcoat is constructed of machine-knitted fabric threaded with string to create a unique "natural" garment.

ELSPETH KEMP
(top right)
Suede binding with an unusual line frames the embroidered panel of this crossover style waistcoat.

GAYNOR KIRBY *(top centre)*
Tudor textiles inspired this
delicate design.

HILARY MORE *(above)*
The fabric for this waistcoat is

**GILDA BROWN AND
SHELAGH O'GORMAN**
(right)

VERA MORGAN
(far right)

SILK PAINTED WAISTCOATS

Fabric painted waistcoats can be as subtle or as bold as the designer chooses. Translucent watercolour effects show up best on white silk, while opaque paints can be painted over a dark fabric.

ALISON BELL
(left)
This child's waistcoat is decorated with animal characters from favourite stories, hand-painted on silk, then highlighted with gold pen.

CATHERINE CROWTHER
(centre)
Pale yellow painted silk provides a foil for the stencilled sun and moon images which are highlighted in gold.

CATHERINE CROWTHER
(top)
A floral design in pastel shades is painted on silk using a batik wax-resist technique.

✿ ✿ ✿ ✿ ✿ ✿ ✿ ✿ ✿ ✿ ✿ ✿ ✿ ✿ ✿ ✿ ✿

SALLY CUNNINGHAM
(above)
Randomly painted strips of silk
are patched together and woven
into an openwork construction.
Machine embroidery secures
and highlights each strip.

ALISON BELL
(left centre)
These bands of colour have been
painted onto silk to resemble
rock strata, creating a fantasy
landscape for a host of
humorous animal outlines.

SUSIE MOORE
(right centre)
A few large images and clear
colours combine in this discreet
but amusing painted tea cup
waistcoat.

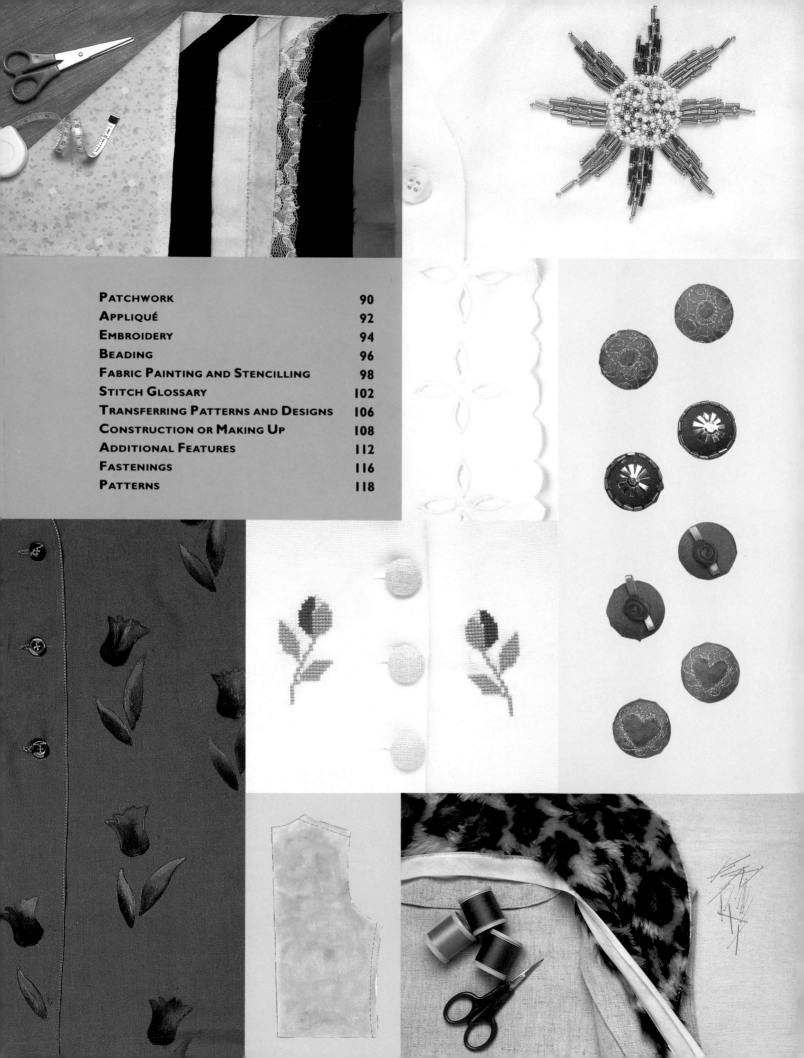

TECHNIQUES AND PATTERNS

IN PATCHWORK SMALL PIECES OF CLOTH ARE CUT INTO REGULAR SHAPES AND JOINED TOGETHER EITHER BY HAND OR MACHINE STITCHING. THE PIECES USED CAN BE IN MATCHING TONES OR CONTRASTING COLOURS AND THE COMBINED EFFECT OF THE SHAPES AND COLOURS CREATES A WHOLE NEW PIECE OF FABRIC WITH AN INTRICATE DESIGN. PATCHWORK ORIGINATED AS AN ECONOMIC WAY OF PRODUCING LARGE PIECES OF CLOTH FROM RECYCLED MATERIALS.

PATCHWORK

✾ ✾ ✾ ✾ ✾ ✾ ✾ ✾ ✾ ✾ ✾ ✾ ✾ ✾ ✾ ✾ ✾

Some of the oldest examples of patchwork are quilts. They have a geometric design made up of squares, triangles, diamonds and rectangles which were made by simply folding and cutting the fabric. Around the mid-nineteenth century templates were introduced which gave rise to more elaborate designs such as the widely used honeycomb pattern.

Materials and Equipment

Any kind of material can be used to make patchwork, but it is easier to work with fabrics of the same thickness. Cotton is the most popular as it is available in a wide variety of colours and designs, keeps its shape and is easy to cut, fold and sew neatly. When fabrics of different weights are sewn together the finer one may tear. It is also more difficult to fold and sew heavy fabric to an exact size, and uneven-sized patches can distort the overall pattern. However, crazy patchwork

takes advantage of these factors. It can be made from a wide variety of pieces in different colours, shapes, weights and textures arranged in a random pattern. The striking effect this produces makes excellent fabric for a waistcoat.

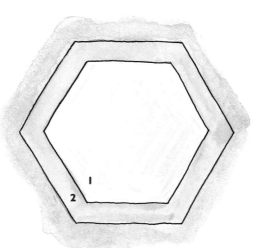

1. paper templates
2. fabric template with 6mm (¼in) seam allowance

ENGLISH PATCHWORK

IN TRADITIONAL ENGLISH PATCHWORK THE FABRIC PIECES ARE TACKED ONTO IDENTICAL PAPER SHAPES SUCH AS HEXAGONS OR DIAMONDS, THEN SEWN TOGETHER TO CREATE A PATTERN.

1 Cut templates 1 and 2 from thin card using a craft knife and cutting board. Cut plenty of paper shapes from clean paper using template 1.

2 To make sure the paper shapes are identical, cut them on a board using a craft knife pressed against the side of the template. Do

not draw round a template and then cut it out as the result will not be accurate. Using template 2, trace fabric shapes on different pieces of material until you think you have enough to make your article. Cut them out accurately with scissors. Check the quantity against the garment pattern by laying the fabric shapes on top. You can plan the arrangement of the colours and work out the pattern at this stage.

3 Tack a paper shape onto the back of each fabric shape, turning the raw edges to the reverse, tacking them down as you go.

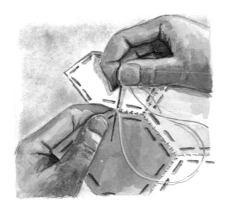

4 Take backed fabric shapes, hold them face to face and stitch along one side overcasting with close firm stitches.

Continue sewing the shapes together, building up the pattern in this manner until the patchwork is the size needed for the article you wish to make. You can now use the patchwork like an ordinary piece of fabric, but when you have finished sewing the article remove all tacking stitches and take out the paper.

AMERICAN PATCHWORK

AMERICAN PATCHWORK QUILTS WERE OFTEN PIECED TOGETHER FROM SQUARE BLOCKS. THE BLOCKS WERE EASILY PORTABLE AND COULD BE STORED UNTIL THERE WERE SUFFICIENT TO MAKE THE FINISHED ARTICLE. MANY QUILTS WERE MADE COMMUNALLY IN THIS WAY. QUICK METHODS FOR ASSEMBLING THE BLOCKS WERE DEVISED AND BLOCK PATCHWORK CAN ALSO BE DONE EASILY ON A SEWING MACHINE.

1 Draw out a block pattern using graph paper. Divide the block into equal squares. Further divide the alternate blocks into two triangles. You will need only two templates: 1 – the full square and 2 – the triangle. Transfer the shapes from your block diagram onto card and cut them out.

2 Choose three contrasting or, if you prefer, toning fabrics and cut the required shapes adding on a 6 mm (¼ inch) seam allowance all round each shape.

3 Machine stitch the triangles together to form a square then stitch each square together to make up one block using the 6 mm (¼ inch) seam allowance.

Alternate the colours in each block, then machine all the blocks together until you have enough fabric to make two symmetrical waistcoat fronts.

4 Press all seams open and trim any excess bulk wherever several seams meet. Press seams between light and dark colours towards the dark fabric as they may show through the light fabric.

✿ **TIP** *Remember a smaller block is best for a small garment like a waistcoat as it has to be repeated over a fairly small area.*

APPLIQUÉ IS THE TECHNIQUE OF STITCHING CUT-OUT SHAPES ONTO A FINISHED BACKGROUND TO CREATE A RAISED, DECORATIVE MOTIF ON CLOTHING OR FURNISHINGS. APPLIQUÉ MOTIFS CAN BE STITCHED ON BY HAND USING PLAIN SEWING, OR AN EMBROIDERY STITCH TO GIVE A DECORATIVE EDGING. OR THEY MAY BE SEWN ON BY MACHINE AND THIS OPERATION MAY BE COMBINED WITH MACHINE EMBROIDERY TOO.

APPLIQUÉ

✲ ✲ ✲ ✲ ✲ ✲ ✲ ✲ ✲ ✲ ✲ ✲ ✲ ✲ ✲ ✲

Originally, appliqué was a functional technique – for sewing patches on knees and elbows, or attaching badges or labels. But now it is used extensively for decorating garments, quilts, cushions and other objects.

There are various types of appliqué including reverse appliqué, known as mola work. Bold, simple designs can be stitched straight on. For more complex ones, involving very small motifs, fusible bonding is used. Shapes can be interfaced first to give them more body or to stop the fabric fraying too much. Fusible bonding also allows shapes to be trimmed very precisely

then heat pressed into position before being stitched. Small pieces of fabric, stitched on and then deliberately frayed, exploit the texture of a raw edge.

Appliqué can also be quilted, or decorated further with different embroidery stitches such as buttonhole stitch. For a very elaborate effect, beads, sequins, feathers and other objects can be sewn onto the appliqué motif. It also provides the ideal means for attaching initials to personalize a garment.

TURNED EDGE APPLIQUÉ

THIS IS THE MOST COMMON METHOD OF APPLIQUÉ WHICH HAS LONG BEEN USED ON QUILTS, GARMENTS, FABRICS WHICH FRAY, AND FOR PADDED MOTIFS.

1 Cut out each pattern piece including a seam allowance of 6–12 mm (¼–½ in).

2 Tack or bond on interfacing on the reverse to fit the finished size of each piece.

3 Turn the seam allowance under on the reverse side and tack it down. Prepare all the appliqué shapes like this.

4 Stretch the required area of the background fabric over an embroidery frame and pin and tack each appliqué shape in place, working from the background to foreground if they are superimposed.

5 Slipstitch along the edge of each shape with tiny stitches close to the edge of the motif. Remove the tacking stitches. Avoid pressing an appliqué motif as it tends to flatten it and spoil the effect.

MACHINE APPLIQUÉ

MACHINE APPLIQUÉ IS QUICK TO DO AND ADDED TEXTURE CAN BE PROVIDED BY COMBINING THE APPLIQUÉ WITH MACHINE EMBROIDERY.

1 Iron a sheet of fusible bonding onto the reverse of appliqué fabric. Trace and then cut out the motifs, peel off the backing sheet and use an iron to bond the motifs onto the background fabric.

2 Machine around the motif outline. Use satin stitch or another of the automatic machine stitches. For a free effect, you can attach the motifs with machine embroidery lines and scrolls. The bonding will help prevent fraying.

PERSIAN APPLIQUÉ

THIS NINETEENTH-CENTURY TECHNIQUE IMITATES DETAILED EMBROIDERY BY ATTACHING TRIMMED PRINTED MOTIFS TO A BACKGROUND FABRIC.

1 Cut out the printed motifs and bond them in place.

2 Secure the motifs with satin stitch by hand or machine or by using another hand embroidery stitch, stab stitching or overcast stitching.

DECORATIVE EDGES

DECORATIVE STITCHES CAN ALSO BE USED TO FINISH THE EDGES ON EITHER TURNED EDGE OR RAW EDGE APPLIQUÉ.

1 Suitable stitches are cretan stitch, feather stitch and buttonhole stitch. (See Stitch Glossary pp.102–5.) These stitches should enhance the design but are not intended to form the focal point.

EMBROIDERY CAN ADD EXTRA ORNAMENT TO ANY SEWING PROJECT WHETHER IT STARTS OUT AS PLAIN OR PAINTED FABRIC, PATCHWORK OR APPLIQUÉ. HAND EMBROIDERING A LARGE PIECE OF FABRIC, SUCH AS A GARMENT, TAKES A LONG TIME, BUT WITH A MODERN SEWING MACHINE BEAUTIFUL DESIGNS CAN BE COMPLETED VERY QUICKLY. IF YOU DO NOT HAVE A SUITABLE MACHINE, ALL THE HAND EMBROIDERY STITCHES, AS WELL AS THOSE FOR PLAIN SEWING, ARE ILLUSTRATED IN THE STITCH GLOSSARY.

EMBROIDERY

For machine embroidery you need an electric sewing machine with a removable spool case, so that you can adjust the tension if using thick embroidery thread, and a "feed dog" that can either be lowered or covered with a plate. You will also need a selection of machine needles in various sizes (the thicker the thread and fabric, the bigger the needle required) and an embroidery ring to hold the fabric taut.

It takes time to get used to manipulating the fabric and controlling the speed for embroidery so always practise on a scrap of fabric first.

Experiment with the tension setting when practising each type of stitch. The presser foot bar must always be lowered to activate the tension, even when the presser foot itself is removed, as in free embroidery.

USING A FRAME

UNLESS YOU ARE VERY EXPERIENCED ALWAYS USE AN EMBROIDERY FRAME FOR MACHINE EMBROIDERY. A RING FRAME IS IDEAL FOR SMALLER PIECES OF WORK.

1 Before you begin bind the inner ring with strips of cotton. This will protect the delicate embroidery stitching as you work across the fabric areas.

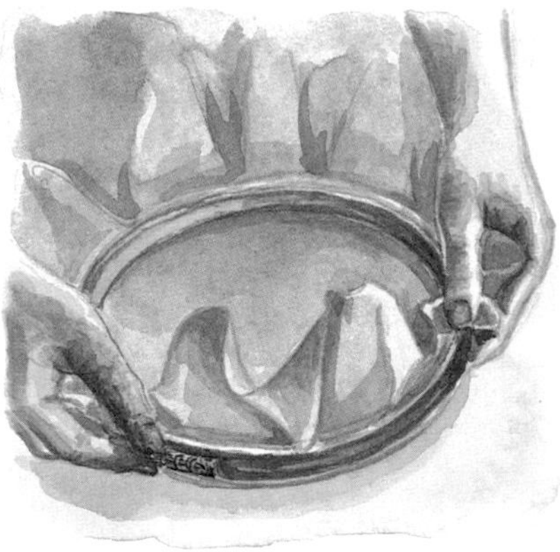

2 Lay the outer ring down, place the fabric on top, face downward, and insert inner ring. Tighten the fabric and screw up the outer ring. The inner ring should stand *slightly* below the outer ring to allow the fabric to contact the machine bed.

USING THE PRESSER FOOT

SOME MACHINES ARE EQUIPPED WITH A TRANSPARENT PRESSER FOOT SO THAT THE STITCHING CAN BE SEEN MORE CLEARLY.

1 Thread the machine as normal and begin straight stitching backwards and forwards. Use different thread and stitch lengths to create texture. Build up rows of vertical and horizontal lines to create solid colour.

2 Adjust the stitch width to achieve a zigzag stitch and the stitch length to achieve satin stitch. Experiment by widening and narrowing the width to create dots, blocks and triangles in satin stitch.

✿ **TIP** *Use the twin needles to sew parallel lines in similar or contrasting threads to create textural lines.*

TACKING FOOT

1 Surface loops are created using the tacking foot and by adjusting the stitch width. These are good for landscape effects and textural areas.

FREE EMBROIDERY

ALWAYS USE A FRAME FOR THIS, THE MOST CREATIVE WAY OF STITCHING.

1 For free machining you must disengage the feed dog, reduce the stitch width to zero and remove the presser foot.

2 Slide in the framed fabric and *lower* the presser foot bar. Turn the wheel to insert the needle, then raise it and pull the bobbin thread through. Pull the thread to the left side and insert the needle again before pressing the motor drive slowly.

3 Move the frame about gently to create an area of stitching. Practise "doodling" and writing names before progressing to motifs and all-over patterns and textures.

4 Adjust the stitch width to produce a free zigzag stitch. Move the hoop slowly for satin stitch, faster for zigzag wavy lines.

Whip stitch and cable stitch can also be done by machine (see Stitch Glossary, pp.102–5).

BEADS CAN BE USED TO CREATE A RICH, TEXTURED DECORATION ON GARMENTS. THIS CENTURY, BEADING WAS USED MOST DRAMATICALLY ON 1920S "FLAPPER" DRESSES WHERE DENSE ROWS OF GLASS BEADS CAUGHT AND REFLECTED THE ELECTRIC LIGHT WHICH WAS NEW AT THAT TIME. IN VICTORIAN ENGLAND BLACK JET BEADS WERE USED AS SOBER BUT LUSTROUS DECORATION ON MOURNING WEAR, A FASHION LED BY QUEEN VICTORIA AFTER THE DEATH OF PRINCE ALBERT.

BEADING

✿ ✿ ✿ ✿ ✿ ✿ ✿ ✿ ✿ ✿ ✿ ✿ ✿ ✿ ✿ ✿

A good selection of beads can now be found in most craft shops. There are many types including rocailles, artificial seed pearls, tiny tube-shaped bugle beads, floral hand-painted ceramic beads, sequins and many others.

Materials and Equipment

Sewing on fine beads usually requires special beading needles which are very long and fine. They are fragile and tend to bend so you may have to replace them frequently. A strong thread is also needed – use cotton or polyester. The thread should be strengthened further by pulling it through a beeswax block. This will also prevent the thread from twisting.

Any fabric can be beaded although lightweight fabrics may need extra backing. An embroidery hoop can be used to hold the fabric taut when beading.

EMBROIDERING WITH INDIVIDUAL BEADS

ALTHOUGH IT IS TIME-CONSUMING TO SEW ON BEADS INDIVIDUALLY, THE END RESULT IS CERTAINLY WORTH WHILE AND COULD RESULT IN AN ORDINARY GARMENT BECOMING AN HEIRLOOM.

1 For fine beads you will need a fine beading needle and invisible thread or a colour to match the background fabric. Knot the end of the thread and insert the needle into the right side of the fabric. Make two to three stitches on the wrong side to secure the thread firmly and bring the needle out again beside the knot.

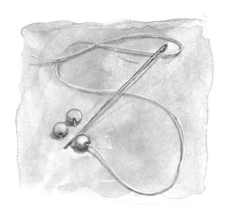

2 Thread the bead and reinsert the needle close to the point where it emerged.

3 Bring the needle up at the right position for the centre of the next bead, thread the bead, reinsert the needle and continue. Make a back stitch every third bead to secure the arrangement.

BUGLE BEADS

BUGLE BEADS ARE TINY, TUBE-SHAPED BEADS THAT CAN BE LAID END TO END TO CREATE A LUSTROUS, FLEXIBLE PIPING OR CORDING EFFECT. THEY CAN ALSO BE USED TO MAKE TINY STAR-SHAPED FLOWERS OR SUNBURST DESIGNS.

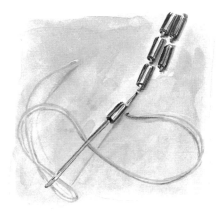

1 Sew on bugle beads in the same way as individual beads, but always make a backstitch through each bead to secure it firmly.

✾ **TIP** *For theatrical costumes dense beading can be produced quickly by using strong fabric glue. You could also use this method for a garment that will not be washed or subjected to much wear and tear.*

COUCHING

IT IS EASIER TO WORK OUT A DESIGN WHEN YOU HAVE A GROUP OF BEADS ALREADY THREADED TOGETHER. COUCHING SAVES TIME BECAUSE IT IS QUICKER TO THREAD SEVERAL BEADS AT ONE GO, THAN INDIVIDUAL BEADS AT INTERVALS.

1 Knot the end of the thread, bring it through to the surface of the fabric and thread on the beads.

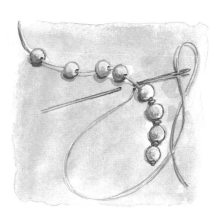

2 Use a *separate* needle and thread to make a small overcast stitch across the bead thread as close as possible to the first bead. Slide each bead up in turn and secure with the couching thread. When finished secure the couching thread on the reverse, then the beaded thread.

✾ **TIP** *You can use a decorative thread and french knots in between beads for added colour. (See French Knots pages 102–5.)*

ATTACHING FRINGING

BEADED FRINGES MAKE A DRAMATIC AND DECORATIVE EDGE TO EVENING WEAR.

1 Decide on the finished length of the fringe and cut the thread to twice the length plus a 10 cm (4 in) allowance for sewing and knotting the thread.

2 Thread the beads by taking a single thread through the bottom bead then the double thread through the remainder of the beads. Stitch the loose ends through the fabric and finish by knotting ends together.

3 Alternatively, knot the thread and bring the needle through to the right side of the fabric, thread on enough beads to make the complete bead loop, then reinsert the needle next to the point where it emerged. Oversew the ends a few times and finish off on the reverse.

HAND PAINTING ON FABRIC IS AN ANCIENT CRAFT FIRST PRACTISED ON NATURAL SILK IN THE FAR EAST. THE SHEEN OF FINE SILK COMBINES WITH THE TRANSLUCENT COLOURS OF FABRIC PAINTS TO CREATE A BEAUTIFUL EFFECT. MODERN FABRIC PAINTS WITH SPECIAL APPLICATORS CAN BE USED TO CREATE A WIDE VARIETY OF FINISHES, RANGING FROM A METALLIC LOOK TO THREE-DIMENSIONAL RAISED EFFECTS AND BEADING. FABRIC PAINTS ARE OFTEN USED IN CONJUNCTION WITH STENCILS.

FABRIC PAINTING AND STENCILLING

Whereas Chinese silk painting has remained an unbroken tradition, in Europe the popularity of painted fabric was replaced by the demand for printed fabric as printing techniques developed. Fabric painting is now enjoying a revival, particularly among craft workers, and colour-fast fabric dyes which can be fixed with a hot iron are widely available.

In addition to silk, some synthetic fabrics, cotton and linen can be used for fabric painting provided the correct type of fabric paint is used.

The paints can be applied in a wide variety of ways using brushes, sponges, pens, sprays, stamp shapes, squeegee and rollerball nozzles. Resist techniques allow areas of colour to be applied without the colours running together or bleeding. Other methods, such as the salt technique, take advantage of the effects produced by colours mixing and flowing together.

Designs can be done freehand, but several techniques involve the use of stencils to apply different colours to particular areas of the design. Stencils are particularly useful for producing repeat patterns.

Fabric painting

All fabric painting techniques require similar basic equipment:

- Wash and dry fabric before painting to allow for shrinkage and colour fading.
- It is best to use a stretcher frame to hold the fabric taut.
- Use a range of brushes of different thicknesses for applying colour washes or fine detail.
- A thinner is needed for oil-based paints, or a jar of clean water for water-based paints.
- Rags are used to clean and dry brushes between colours.
- Practise the technique on scraps of the fabric.
- Collect examples and sketches of design ideas to copy, trace or develop from your imagination.
- To "fix" the colours and finish off painted fabric either press with a hot iron or steam as directed by the paint manufacturer's instructions.

PAINTING ON SILK: RESIST METHOD

THIS ALLOWS DETAILED AREAS TO BE DRAWN AND STRONG AREAS OF COLOUR TO BE PLACED NEXT TO EACH OTHER WITHOUT "BLEEDING".

1 Stretch the fabric across the frame and pin in place. Sketch the design lightly onto the silk with a soluble fabric marker pen, or place a drawing directly underneath.

2 Trace over the outlines on the silk using a gutta pen (clear, gold or silver) and leave to dry. Clean the nozzle with a tissue frequently to stop blobs forming. The gutta acts as barrier between the areas of colour.

3 Fill in the areas with liquid silk paint. Begin in the middle of a shape and work nearly to the gutta outline. The paint will spread on its own. You can build the colour gradually to a strong intensity, leaving it to dry between "coats".

PAINTING ON SILK: WATER-COLOUR METHOD

THIS TECHNIQUE DOES NOT USE OUTLINER, INSTEAD THE COLOURS ARE ENCOURAGED TO FLOW INTO ONE ANOTHER. THE TECHNIQUE CAN ALSO BE ADAPTED FOR USE WITH OIL-BASED PAINTS, USING A THINNER TO MAKE THE COLOURS FLOW.

1 Brush the fabric with water (or thinner if using oil-based paints) according to the manufacturer's instructions, then quickly apply the paints onto the wet silk. Start with lighter tones working up or down a panel to darker tones. Add detail by painting in shapes such as trees on a landscape background. Add more fine detail as the work begins to dry as the colours will not flow as much.

2 Brush on water (or thinner) to break up areas that appear too solid. Dark watermark edges will appear, but these can be considered part of the final design.

PAINTING ON SILK: SALT METHOD

THIS TECHNIQUE CAN BE USED TO PRODUCE A STRIKING EFFECT ON ITS OWN, OR IT CAN BE COMBINED WITH EITHER THE RESIST OR WATERCOLOUR TECHNIQUES.

1 Scatter salt over damp, freshly painted areas of the fabric. The salt absorbs the water and pigment so a marbled and clouded effect results. Leave the salt and silk to dry before brushing the salt off.

Table salt and coarse sea salt produce different effects. To make it more effective, dry the salt in a warm oven before use.

EMBOSSED FABRIC PAINTS

EMBOSSED FABRIC PAINTS CAN BE USED ON THEIR OWN FOR A CORDED OR BEADED EFFECT, OR ON TOP OF ALREADY PAINTED FABRIC TO CREATE A RAISED,

3-D EFFECT. THESE PAINTS COME IN A SQUEEZY TUBE WITH A SPECIAL NOZZLE.

1 Squeeze the tube gently but firmly and draw either smooth flowing lines or a series of dots. Colours can be placed next to each other as they should not run. Leave to dry overnight.

CREME PAINTS

CREME FABRIC PAINT USUALLY COMES IN SMALL JARS AND IS OIL-BASED SO YOU WILL ALSO REQUIRE THINNER.

1 Mark the design outline onto the fabric using a soluble fabric marker pen. Pour the thinner into a shallow container and with the creme paint begin by painting the light areas within a shape, then the darker tones. Blend the tones as you go, thinning the paint colours as required. When the paint is touch-dry add highlights and details.

STENCILLING

STENCILLING IS ASSOCIATED MAINLY WITH DECORATIVE WALL BORDERS, BUT MANY TEXTILE DESIGNERS ALSO USE STENCILS. IN THIS TECHNIQUE THE DRAWINGS ARE STYLIZED, A COMMON FEATURE OF FOLK ART, AND THIS MAKES REPEAT DESIGNS EASY.

THE BASIC TOOLS REQUIRED ARE A SELECTION OF STENCIL PAINTS (NOT CRAYONS), STENCIL BRUSHES IN A FEW SIZES, SOME PAPER TOWELS, AN ERASER, MASKING TAPE AND A PRE-CUT STENCIL DESIGN ON CARD OR ACETATE.

1 To make your own stencil design lay a sheet of thick acetate over a sketch of your design and trace the outlines, keeping it as simple as possible. Lay the acetate on the cutting mat and cut out the shapes cleanly with a craft knife. Leave narrow "bridges" connecting the inner parts of the design to the edge of the outline. You can make separate stencils for different coloured areas of the design if it is very detailed. Alternatively, you can mask off the unwanted "holes".

Make a central registration mark on your design that won't be cut out and mark this point on each stencil sheet so that you can overlay exactly each time.

2 Tape the stencil to the fabric. Load your brush with the first colour, and remove excess paint. Brush to the outline of the stencil shape with a circular motion, keeping the brush vertical. With large cut-out areas you can add shading and highlights. Allow the first colour to dry and clean the stencil before applying the second colour. Mask off unwanted areas, or use separate stencils for designs which combine different colours.

3 Leave the fabric to dry for 24 hours before heat setting it with a cool iron and a dry pressing cloth or as directed by the paint manufacturer.

THERE ARE MANY TYPES OF HAND-EMBROIDERY STITCHES. SOME, SUCH AS DAISY STITCH, ARE MAINLY DECORATIVE, WHILE SOME PERFORM A FUNCTION AS WELL, SUCH AS HERRINGBONE WHICH CAN BE USED TO OVERSEW A HEM.

STITCH GLOSSARY

✺ ✺ ✺ ✺ ✺ ✺ ✺ ✺ ✺ ✺ ✺ ✺ ✺ ✺ ✺ ✺

Freestyle embroidery

Freestyle embroidery can be done on almost any fabric with any thread, and by experimenting with weights of fabric and thread combinations you can produce wonderful patterns and textures.

Needles

You will need a variety of embroidery needles in various sizes to allow for the different types of thread and fabric, but for a novice, 2/3 strands of stranded cotton and a No 6 or 7 crewel embroidery needle are the easiest to handle.

Use an embroidery hoop for large pieces of work. To prevent the hoop snagging fabric or the embroidery, bind the inner ring with strips of cotton fabric first.

RUNNING STITCH

A simple in-and-out stitch normally used to make gathers.

TACKING STITCH

A long-and-short running stitch used to hold pieces of fabric together temporarily before machining or fine sewing.

OVERCASTING

This stitch is used to finish edges, particularly if there is a danger of the material fraying. Work from either direction, taking the thread over the edge of the fabric. Do not pull the thread too tightly.

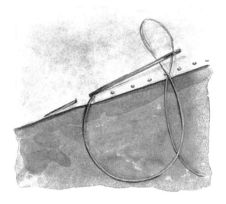

STAB STITCH

Bring the needle through to the right side. Stab the needle through the material to form a tiny stitch. Also known as prick stitch, it should be almost invisible on the right side.

SLIP STITCH

Bring the needle through to the right side. Insert it and then bring back up to form a neat line of small stitches.

BACKSTITCH

Bring the thread through on the stitch line, then take a small backward stitch through the fabric. Bring the needle through again a little in front of the first stitch, take another backward stitch to fill in the gap. Keep the stitches small and even. This is also known as Running Backstitch. It is good for outlining and adding detail. It can also be used for handsewing seams.

STEM STITCH

Work from left to right (if you are right-handed) taking small, regular backstitches that slightly overlap as you stitch along the line of the design. The thread should always emerge on the same side of the previous stitch so that all the overlaps lie in the same direction.

Stem stitch is used for flower stems and outlines. It can also be used as a filling stitch by working rows of stem stitch close together within a shape.

WHIPPING STITCH

By weaving or "whipping" a second, contrasting thread through a running stitch, a very attractive plaited effect can be created.

This can be done very effectively by machine. Use a fine embroidery thread in the bobbin and a firm cotton sewing thread on top. Tighten the top tension and slightly slacken the bottom tension. Stitch quickly but move the hoop slowly. The bobbin thread will cord and cover the top thread. This is most effective with contrasting colours and can be used as a decorative top stitch on existing garments.

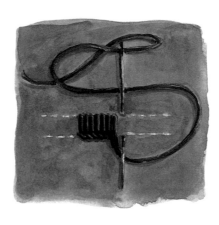

BUTTONHOLE STITCH

Bring the thread out on the lower line, insert the needle in position on the upper line, taking a straight downward stitch with the thread looped under the needle point. Pull the thread through to tighten the loop and repeat, keeping the stitches very close together. The rolled edge created by the linked loops becomes the edge of the buttonhole. Always cut the buttonhole slit *after* completing the buttonhole stitching.

Most machines will do a very good buttonhole stitch with professional results.

A purely decorative version can be created by spacing the stitches more widely as in *Blanket Stitch*. It can be worked round an appliqué shape and is also used in cutwork where the looped edge defines the area of fabric to be cut away.

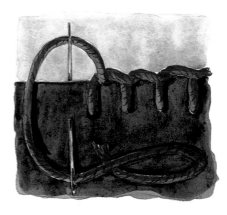

BLANKET STITCH

Work this like buttonhole stitch with the stitches spaced out.

It was traditionally used for edging woollen cloth or blankets and gives an attractive "folk" image to garments. This is also known as Detached Buttonhole Stitch.

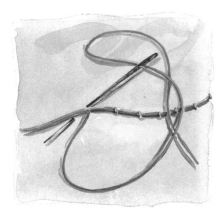

COUCHING

To "couch" a thread, lay it along the line of a design, and with another thread, anchor it down at regular intervals with small stitches through the fabric. The anchoring stitch can be self-coloured and therefore invisible, or a contrasting colour to the laid thread if desired. Varied weights of thread can create an interesting effect.

Couching is used for attaching cord, braid and strings of beads.

SATIN STITCH

Make rows of adjacent straight stitches, working them closely together across the shape. In a small area, such as a tiny leaf or petal, the stitches can go from edge to edge of the outline. To fill in large areas with satin stitch, make stitches of

different lengths on the first row, then fill in with more for the second row. This disguises the "joins" and gives the whole area a satin finish. On its own, this is known as Long-and-Short Stitch.

On a machine, satin stitch is done using a zigzag stitch set to almost zero stitch length.

Satin stitch is the most solid filling stitch. The shape can be padded to give a raised effect by first putting some running stitches (small evenly spaced stitches) across the area at right angles to the satin stitches. Care must be taken to keep the edges even.

CABLE STITCH

Cable stitch is a variation of chain stitch (right). It is worked in a similar way to ordinary chain stitch but in this case the thread is twisted around the needle after each chain loop, and before it enters the fabric. This makes an intervening link between the chains. The stitch follows curved lines well and makes a good filling stitch when worked solidly.

DAISY STITCH

Start by making a loop in the same way as for chain stitch, but fasten down the top of each loop with a tiny anchoring stitch over the petal tip. Begin the next loop alongside.

This stitch can be worked singly or in groups to form flower petals, hence the name daisy. Vary the size of the petals for a realistic effect.

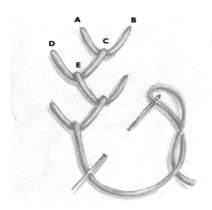

FEATHER STITCH

Bring the needle out at the centre top, hold the thread down with the left thumb, insert the needle a little to the right at B on the same level and bring the point up at C below and between A and B, keeping the thread under the needle point. Next, insert the needle at D and bring it up at E, looping the thread under the point. Then in at F and up at G, imitating the stitch at B and C. Work these two movements alternately to create the two sides of the "feather".

This stitch makes a delicate border and is very useful in floral designs.

HERRINGBONE STITCH

Bring the needle out on the lower line at the left side and insert on the upper line a little to the right. Make a small stitch to the left, keeping the thread *below* the needle. Insert the needle on the lower line a little to the right and take a small stitch to the left with the thread *above* the needle. Repeat this sequence along the line, keeping the spacing even.

Herringbone is useful as a decorative stitch or for catching and finishing a hem or raw edge.

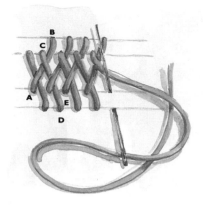

CRETAN STITCH

This is worked in a similar way to herringbone stitch and forms a zig-zag line.

Bring the thread through from the back of the fabric at A, then insert the needle vertically downwards, in at B and up at C, keeping the thread under the needle. Next, the needle goes in at D, below, and up at E, vertically above D. Proceed along the line, spacing the stitches closely for Closed Cretan Stitch, or apart for Open Cretan Stitch.

It can also be worked freely to create textured effects like grass, and closed up to produce a central plait. This is a useful filling stitch.

CHAIN STITCH

Starting with a knot on the end of the thread insert the needle from the back of the fabric, bring the thread through and hold the working thread down with the left thumb. Reinsert the needle very close to the place where it emerged and bring the point out a short distance along the line or curve so that the working thread loops under the needle point. Pull the thread through gently. Again, insert the needle at the place it last emerged and make another loop. Continue making a chain of loops.

This is a good stitch for working around curved shapes.

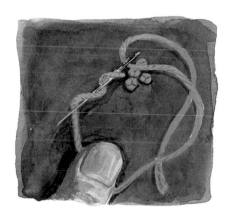

FRENCH KNOTS

Bring the thread out at the required position, hold the thread down with the left thumb and encircle the thread twice with the needle. Still keeping the looped thread taut, twist the needle back to the starting point and insert it close to the point where it first emerged. Pull the thread through to the back and overstitch to secure a single French Knot, or work several in succession.

French Knots are useful for tiny flower centres and can be used as a filling stitch.

THERE ARE MANY WAYS OF TRANSFERRING DESIGNS TO FABRIC: FREEHAND DRAWING WITH CHALK; TRACING PAPER AND PENCIL, WHICH CAN BE ERASED ON STRONG FABRICS; DRESSMAKER'S CARBON COPYING PAPER; TACKING ROUND THE OUTLINE; DRAWING ROUND TEMPLATES OR STENCILS; STAMPING; PRICKING AND POUNCING; IRON-ON TRANSFERS. THE METHOD CHOSEN DEPENDS ON THE TYPES OF FABRIC BEING USED, THE DESIGN AND THE DECORATION: THREAD, BEADS, PAINT, APPLIQUÉD FABRIC AND SO ON.

TRANSFERRING PATTERNS AND DESIGNS

❋ ❋ ❋ ❋ ❋ ❋ ❋ ❋ ❋ ❋ ❋ ❋ ❋ ❋ ❋ ❋

Some of the transfer methods have disadvantages when used for particular fabrics or designs.

Chalk lines wear off quickly if rubbed. This is useful for guidelines for machine embroidery but is not ideal for hand embroidery.

Dressmaker's carbon paper is a semi-permanent marker so be sure the design positioning is correct before using it. Do not use it for fabric painting as you will be unable to cover up the lines.

More complex designs are unsuitable for tracing out by *tacking* because it would become more time consuming than the project itself.

The traditional method of *enlarging* or *reducing* a design is to use squared grids or graph paper. This can also be done on a good photocopying machine.

TRACING THROUGH THIN FABRIC
When using a transparent or light coloured fabric it is often possible to trace the pattern directly. Lay the fabric on top of the pattern and trace using either pencil, soluble ink, fading ink or tailor's chalk. Move the fabric along and repeat if necessary.

DRESSMAKER'S CARBON PAPER
Dressmaker's carbon paper is similar to typing carbon paper. It is available in several colours suitable for showing up clearly on light or dark fabrics. Lay the paper face down on the right side of your fabric and place the pattern on top. Trace the lines using a dressmaker's tracing wheel.

LIGHTBOX OR WINDOW TRACING
This method allows you to trace directly onto darker fabric. Use masking tape to fix the pattern to the lightbox or a window with bright daylight coming through. Tape the fabric on top, right side up, to keep it taut and in place. Trace the pattern using either pencil, soluble ink, fading ink or tailor's chalk.

TRACING AROUND TEMPLATES

You can buy ready made templates for some designs, or make up your own. Cut out the template in card and lay it on the fabric. Trace the outline using pencil, soluble ink, fading ink or tailor's chalk.

IRON-ON TRANSFERS

You can buy ready made iron-on transfers or design your own using a transfer pencil and tracing paper. Draw or trace the design onto the tracing paper in normal pencil. Go over the design with a transfer pencil on the reverse. Place the transfer face down on the right side of the fabric, then press with a warm iron.

TRACING AND TACKING

Trace the design onto tissue paper and pin it to the fabric. Tack around the design. Tear away the tissue paper carefully to leave the stitched outline. If the tacking is not covered by the design remove it on completion of the work.

PRICKING AND POUNCING

Trace the design onto tracing paper and turn it to the reverse. Use a medium needle to prick holes close together along the design lines. Turn the paper the correct way up and place onto fabric. Rub crushed dressmaker's chalk over the lines of holes using cotton wool. This leaves a fine dotted line of chalk which is easily brushed away later.

ENLARGING OR REDUCING A DESIGN

THERE ARE TWO BASIC METHODS FOR ENLARGING OR REDUCING DESIGNS. BOTH ARE EASY, BUT GRIDS ARE MORE TIME-CONSUMING.

PHOTOCOPYING

With a good photocopying machine you can not only copy the chosen pattern or motif but also enlarge or reduce it to the required size for your project.

GRIDS

1 To enlarge a sketched design of your own, carefully draw a grid of equal squares over the original pattern.

2 Draw a second grid on another sheet of paper using the same number of squares, either larger or smaller than the original ones depending on whether you need to enlarge or reduce the design.

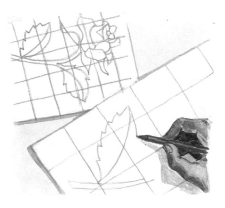

3 Copy the main lines of the first design onto the second grid. The squares make it easy to position the lines. Use this method to scale up the waistcoat patterns given.

THE PROJECTS IN THIS BOOK INCLUDE BOTH ENTIRELY NEW, HOME-MADE WAISTCOATS AND TECHNIQUES FOR DECORATING EXISTING WAISTCOATS BOUGHT NEW, OR RESCUED FROM THE REJECT PILE. THE MAKING-UP TECHNIQUES GIVEN HERE SHOW HOW TO CONSTRUCT A BASIC WAISTCOAT, WHICH CAN BE USED FOR ANY OF THE PROJECTS, WITH INSTRUCTIONS ON HOW TO ADAPT THE METHOD FOR PARTICULAR DESIGNS AND FABRICS, AS WELL AS GUIDANCE ON ALTERING PATTERN SIZES.

CONSTRUCTION OR MAKING UP

✶ ✶ ✶ ✶ ✶ ✶ ✶ ✶ ✶ ✶ ✶ ✶ ✶ ✶ ✶ ✶

The following instructions describe how to make your own waistcoat from new fabric. Beginning with working out your correct size, the book shows how to make a pattern, cut out the fabric, line and interface economically, and sew up the garment, fitting and altering it if necessary as you go.

Refer to the individual projects for special treatment. For example, the Summer Waistcoat and the Mexican Felt Waistcoat are unlined and have individual decorated edges. The position of darts and pockets must be considered in conjunction with the design, particularly in the Cherub Wedding Waistcoat. And of course you could make your own waistcoat to use with any of the "customizing" projects.

Ideal waistcoats for customizing in your own style and colours can often be found by bargain hunters in secondhand clothes' shops and at sales. Waistcoats from men's suits are worth looking out for. Better still are the handsome garments bought to wear on formal occasions. Well made and of fine fabric, they have usually had very little wear and deserve to be given a new lease of life. A few simple alterations adapted from the pattern-fitting section of the instructions will turn a hand-me-down into a snug fit.

✶ TIP *Male buttonholes: left side of wearer. Female buttonholes: right side of wearer.*

MATERIALS

✵

- Basic sewing equipment
- Sewing machine
- 160 cm (1¾ yd) of lining fabric 114 cm (45 in) wide
- 70 cm (¾ yd) of front fabric 114 cm (45 in) wide
- 70 cm (¾ yd) of fusible interfacing 114 cm (45 in) wide
- Matching sewing thread
- Five cover buttons
- Tailor's chalk or tacking thread
- Waistcoat patterns in the correct size – 1 front, 1 back, 1 belt
- Unless otherwise stated *all* fabric should be pinned and tacked before machine stitching and *all* seams should be pressed open.
- All seam allowances are 15 mm (⅝ in)

MAKING A WAISTCOAT BLOCK PATTERN

1 Select the relevant pieces for the waistcoat you want to make. You will need to copy the front and back, and possibly features such as belts, loops or pockets.

2 To enlarge the pattern you could use a photocopier, but it can also be done on grid paper. You can easily alter the pattern by adding a little extra length at the shoulder seam, or at the sides.

3 On a large sheet of paper, draw up a grid of equal squares. Tape a sheet of tracing paper over the grid and copy the pattern pieces shown in the book, square for square. Cut out the front and back pattern pieces.

4 To avoid wasting fabric, lay the pattern pieces on newspaper, draw round them and cut them out, then pin together a paper version of your waistcoat and try it on to see if the shoulders, side seams or armholes need adjusting.

5 If you plan to use the pattern several times, it is worth cutting a proper template out of card.

TO MAKE UP

SOME PROJECTS INVOLVE MARKING THE FRONTS ONLY BUT NOT CUTTING THEM OUT UNTIL THE DECORATION HAS BEEN APPLIED, SO CHECK THE INSTRUCTIONS BEFORE YOU BEGIN.

thread around all the sides and the darts, remove the pattern piece and cut out the front panels. Lay the centre back edge of the back pattern against the fold of the fabric, mark round and cut out the back piece.

1 Fold the right sides of the fabric together, lay the front pattern on the fabric, parallel to the edges, mark round it with chalk or tacking

2 Cut two more fronts from lining and a back pattern piece from the lining as for the main fabric. Mark the darts. Cut two interfacings using the front pattern piece, again marking the darts. Cut two belt pieces.

3 Iron interfacing to the reverse of the decorated front to stiffen it. Set the machine for straight stitch with a stitch length of 3 or 4. Stitch the darts on the front panels and the lining fronts.

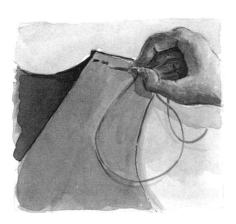

4 Tack and stitch the shoulder seams together for the front and back fabric panels. Then tack and stitch the lining in the same way. Press all seams and darts.

5 Make belt by folding each piece in half, lengthways, stitching one short edge and the long edge. Press, turn right side out, press again.

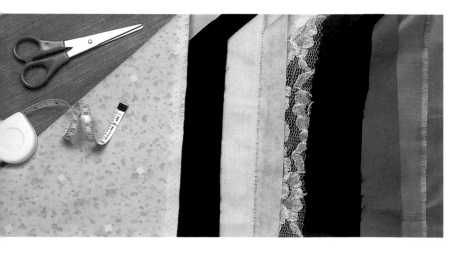

6 Lay the fabric and lining pieces right sides together on a flat surface and pin all around the edges, except for the side seams between the armhole and the lower edge. Tack, then stitch all seams leaving the sides open.

7 Clip into the armhole curves and remove any bulk at seams. Clip excess fabric from the corners. Press seams.

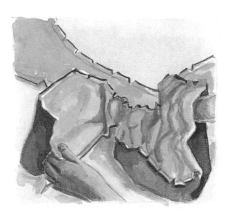

8 Turn the waistcoat right side out by pulling the fronts through the shoulder tunnel and out through the open side edge of the back. Press carefully all around the edges.

9 Place the fabric side seams right sides together and pin from the armhole to the lower edge, then stitch. Press the lining side seam edges 15 mm (5/8 in) to the inside, pin together and oversew neatly to conceal the raw edges inside.

10 Fold the raw belt edges under 15mm (5/8 in) and press. Place on the back waistcoat approximately 25 cm (10 in) from each side seam. Each belt piece (tier) should face the edge. Top stitch a square on each belt piece to fix in place. The ties are knotted together when the waistcoat is worn.

11 If wished, make buttonholes by using either a programmed machine stitch, zigzag stitch, or handsew them using buttonhole stitch. Remember that you do not cut the buttonhole slit until the stitching is finished. Practise on a spare piece of fabric first. The buttonhole should be slightly larger than the finished size of the button. You can cover the buttons with matching fabric and attach to the opposite front to correspond with the buttonholes. Alternatively, use bought buttons.

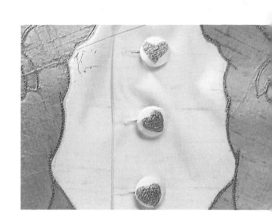

VARIOUS FEATURES CAN BE ADDED TO A WAISTCOAT SUCH AS A HALF-BELT, SIDE VENTS, POCKETS OR A COLLAR. TRADITIONALLY THE REPOSITORY FOR THE GOLD FOB WATCH, POCKETS ARE NOW OFTEN FOR DECORATION ONLY AND MAY JUST BE FALSE FLAPS OR PIPED EDGING. WHEN WORN OVER A SHIRT, A COLLAR SITS OUTSIDE THE WAISTCOAT. BUT FOR WEARING AS A FASHION GARMENT IN ITS OWN RIGHT, A WAISTCOAT CAN BE FINISHED OFF WITH AN ATTACHED COLLAR MADE IN A MATCHING OR CONTRASTING FABRIC.

ADDITIONAL FEATURES

✵　✵　✵　✵　✵　✵　✵　✵　✵　✵　✵　✵　✵　✵　✵　✵

Pockets can be a useful decorative feature but the type should be selected carefully to suit the decorative technique used. Patch pockets and false flaps are easy to attach, but piped pockets should not be attempted on bulky fabrics or those that have machine embroidery, embossed stencilling, appliqué or patchwork, as it would be very difficult to achieve a flat, neat finish. False pockets are best for waistcoats made of a single layer of fabric as the weight of a real pocket will affect the way the front panels hang. But stronger fabrics and lined waistcoats can have real pouched pockets provided the opening is double stitched to avoid stretching or splitting when in use.

A collar can finish off a waistcoat nicely. Waistcoats were commonly worn over shirts, with the shirt collar sitting outside. So to achieve this look when wearing a waistcoat on its own you may like to attach a collar – permanently, or with easily removable slipstitching or fastenings. Matching or contrasting fabrics can be equally effective.

POCKETS

TO MAKE A PIPED POCKET YOU WILL NEED TWO MATCHING FABRIC STRIPS. THE POCKET ITSELF IS ACTUALLY A FLAT ENVELOPE ATTACHED TO THE WRONG SIDE OF THE GARMENT.

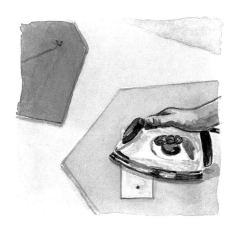

2 Cut pieces of iron-on interfacing 5 cm (2 in) wide and 4 cm (1½ in) longer than the pocket slit marks and iron them onto the wrong side of the waistcoat over the pocket slit marks.

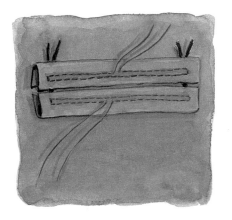

1 Mark the pocket opening on the right side of the fabric then cut two strips of fabric 3 cm (1¼ in) wide and at least 5 cm (2 in) longer than the pocket opening. Iron fusible bonding onto the wrong side of each strip and peel off the paper backing. Fold each strip in half, bonded sides together and press with an iron to bond them together. Trim the strip to twice the required width of the finished piping.

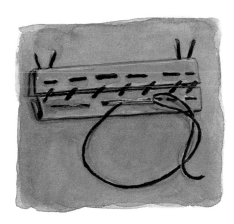

3 On the right side of the fabric, centre the piping strips along the line for the opening. Tack them into position and then tack down the raw edges.

4 Machine backwards and forwards along the centre between the two rows of piping, starting and finishing at the centre point to give a double row of stitches a few mm apart. Remove all tacking threads. Turn the garment wrong side out and slit carefully between the two rows of machining to within 1 cm (⅜ in) of either end.

5 Snip carefully into the corners.

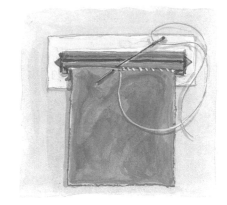

7 Cut two pieces of fabric or lining 3 cm (1¼ in) shorter than the length of piping and approximately 15 cm (6 in) deep. Fold in the raw edge of one piece and hem it to the lower piping, facing right side up. With right sides facing, place the second piece of fabric level with the upper piping. Stitch it to the piping by hand or by machine using a piping foot.

6 Push the piping strips through to the wrong side, and hold them in place by oversewing with tacking stitches on the right side. Fold back the triangles of fabric at either end and press the piping flat. On the right side of the pocket opening stab stitch or machine stitch across the slit ends, or machine stitch all around the opening. This will hold the piping flat.

8 Tack the two pocket pieces together. Mark the outline of the pocket, curving the corners. Stitch around the edge then turn it inside out and zigzag stitch around the raw edges to finish. Make the second pocket to match.

COLLARS

A COLLAR CAN BE THE FOCAL POINT OF A GARMENT AND IT SHOULD BE MADE WITH CARE FOR A PROFESSIONAL RESULT. ALL COLLARS REQUIRE INTERFACING EITHER THROUGHOUT OR IN CERTAIN AREAS FOR STRENGTH AND DEFINITION. USE THE CORRECT WEIGHT OF INTERFACING FOR THE FABRIC. LIGHTWEIGHT FABRICS ARE SUITABLE FOR BOTH FRONT AND BACK OF A COLLAR. BULKY FABRICS SUCH AS THICK WOOL, VELVET OR FUR SHOULD HAVE A BACKING MADE OF LINING MATERIAL. THE FOLLOWING INSTRUCTIONS SHOW HOW TO ATTACH A SHAWL COLLAR.

1 Trace off the paper pattern on p. 126 and pin it in place on the waistcoat. Lengthen or shorten it as shorten it as necessary at this stage. The centre back collar line should meet the centre back line of the waistcoat. When fitted, unpin the pattern.

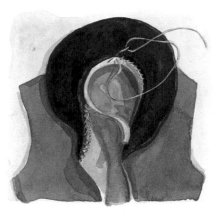

2 Lay the corrected collar pattern on top of the fabric folded with right sides together. Pin the pattern in place and cut round it. Cut matching pieces of interfacing, and lining if required. Trim off 1 cm (³⁄₈ in) all round the interfacing.

4 Place backing and front fabric, right sides together, then pin, tack and stitch the outer collar edge leaving a 15 mm (⁵⁄₈ in) seam allowance. Trim away excess bulk from centre seams then clip small triangular areas from seam allowance, snipping close to but not right up to the stitching line. This will ensure the curved edge lies flat. Turn collar right side out and press flat.

6 Fold over the fabric collar and handstitch it in place over the backing using a small herringbone stitch. Handstitch bias binding over the top of the seam to cover all edges.

3 Iron the interfacing onto the fabric. Pin the collar right sides together at the short edge. Tack then stitch together leaving a 15 mm (⁵⁄₈ in) seam allowance. Press open the seam. Repeat this to make up the back piece from the same fabric, or lining material.

5 Pin the raw backing edge of the collar to the neck edge of the waistcoat, right sides together. Tack and machine stitch using a 15 mm (⁵⁄₈ in) seam allowance. Zigzag the raw edges to prevent fraying.

BUTTONS OR FASTENINGS ADD THE FINISHING TOUCHES TO YOUR WAISTCOAT AND CAN BE AN IMPORTANT FEATURE. IT IS NOT ALWAYS NECESSARY TO MAKE CORRESPONDING BUTTONHOLES AS THE GARMENT CAN BE FASTENED BY OTHER, SIMPLER BUT INVISIBLE MEANS, SUCH AS PATENT FASTENERS. ZIPS, FROG FASTENERS, BUCKLES AND BOWS ARE ALL POSSIBLE DECORATIVE ALTERNATIVES TO BUTTONS.

FASTENINGS

❋　❋　❋　❋　❋　❋　❋　❋　❋　❋　❋　❋　❋　❋　❋　❋

Having designed and decorated your own waistcoat, it can be fun to make a matching set of buttons. Cover button sets, available in all sizes from haberdashers, provide endless opportunities. All you need is small circles of fabric to cover the metal base, then you snap on the metal backing piece and the button is ready to sew on. You can decorate your fabric in dozens of different ways, from machine embroidery to fabric painting, or simply use key motifs selected from a patterned fabric. On a heavily decorated waistcoat, plain covered buttons in a toning colour will work equally well.

Collecting buttons is a fascinating hobby and you may find just the ones for your waistcoat. You might even plan a whole new design around a special set of buttons.

Making your own buttons from scratch is quite easy, using one of the new oven-hardened modelling clays which come in a wide range of colours. You will quickly learn how to mix and blend the colours and create amazing patterns, and they can be made into interesting shapes such as hearts, flowers, animals or butterflies. To finish off the whole outfit you could make a matching set of earrings too.

HEART BUTTONS

MACHINE-EMBROIDERED FABRIC HAS BEEN CUT AWAY TO REVEAL A HEART IN A CONTRASTING COLOUR. THIS DESIGN WILL SUIT ANY PLAIN WAISTCOAT.

1 Set the machine for embroidery. Fill the bobbin with lime thread. Use the gold thread on the top.

2 Stretch the two pieces of fabric into the hoop with the green fabric uppermost. Lay a card template on the fabric and trace around it using chalk or a pen. Repeat across the fabric for the required amount of buttons.

3 Begin by embroidering round the heart three times, then scroll lacey detail around the heart.

4 Embroider all the circles, remove the fabric from the hoop and, using embroidery scissors, snip away the inside of the heart, *only* removing the green fabric, leaving the pink intact. Trim around the cutting edge. Cover the metal buttons as directed by the manufacturer.

ROSEBUD BUTTONS

THESE BUTTONS COULD BE USED TO DECORATE THE ROSEBUD WAISTCOAT FEATURED IN THIS BOOK OR TO ADD A FEMININE TOUCH TO A PLAIN WAISTCOAT.

BEADED BUTTONS

ATTACH GLITTERING BEADS TO BUTTONS FOR A SPARKLY LOOK SUITABLE FOR A PARTY OUTFIT.

1 Using a card template trace the shape onto the fabric, for the required amount of buttons. Trim around the cutting edge and cover button bases.

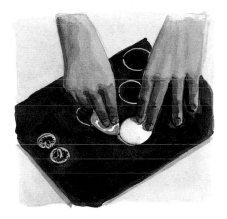

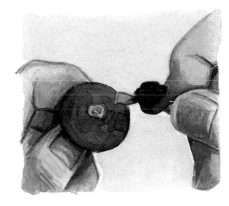

1 Using a card template, trace the shape onto the fabric for the required number of buttons. Trim around the cutting edge and cover the button bases.

2 Place a dot of glue in the centre of the button and one on the base of the rosebud. Press gently together until the glue is set and the bud firmly attached.

2 Place a dot of glue on the centre of the button and on the base of the silver flower. Glue the gold sequin on top, then evenly space the bugle beads around the edge. Leave to set.

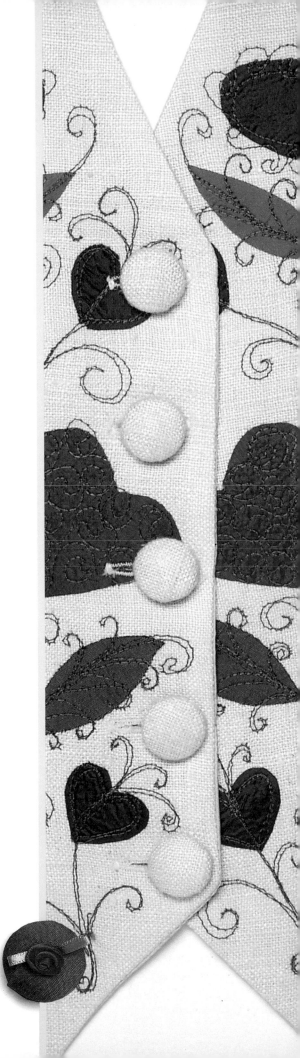

PATTERNS

☼　　☼　　☼　　☼　　☼　　☼　　☼

The patterns given on pp. 118–26 include a
standard ladies' (chest size 85–90 cm (34–36 in)), a
standard gents' (chest size 95–100 cm (38–40 in)) and
some that are specific to a particular project. Certain
designs have different shapes so check the patterns
carefully before you begin. Scale up the patterns by
262 per cent, using either the photocopy or grid
method as described on p. 109. If using the grid method
your new enlarged square size should be 26mm. Make
up the pattern in paper, pinning it in place to ensure a
good fit. To adjust, add or subtract width at the sides
(remember there are tiers at the back which will draw
the waistcoat in). If the waistcoat is too long you can
trim the shoulder seam by up to 25mm (1in) or
you can trim the bottom
edge. You will now have a
personal waistcoat pattern.

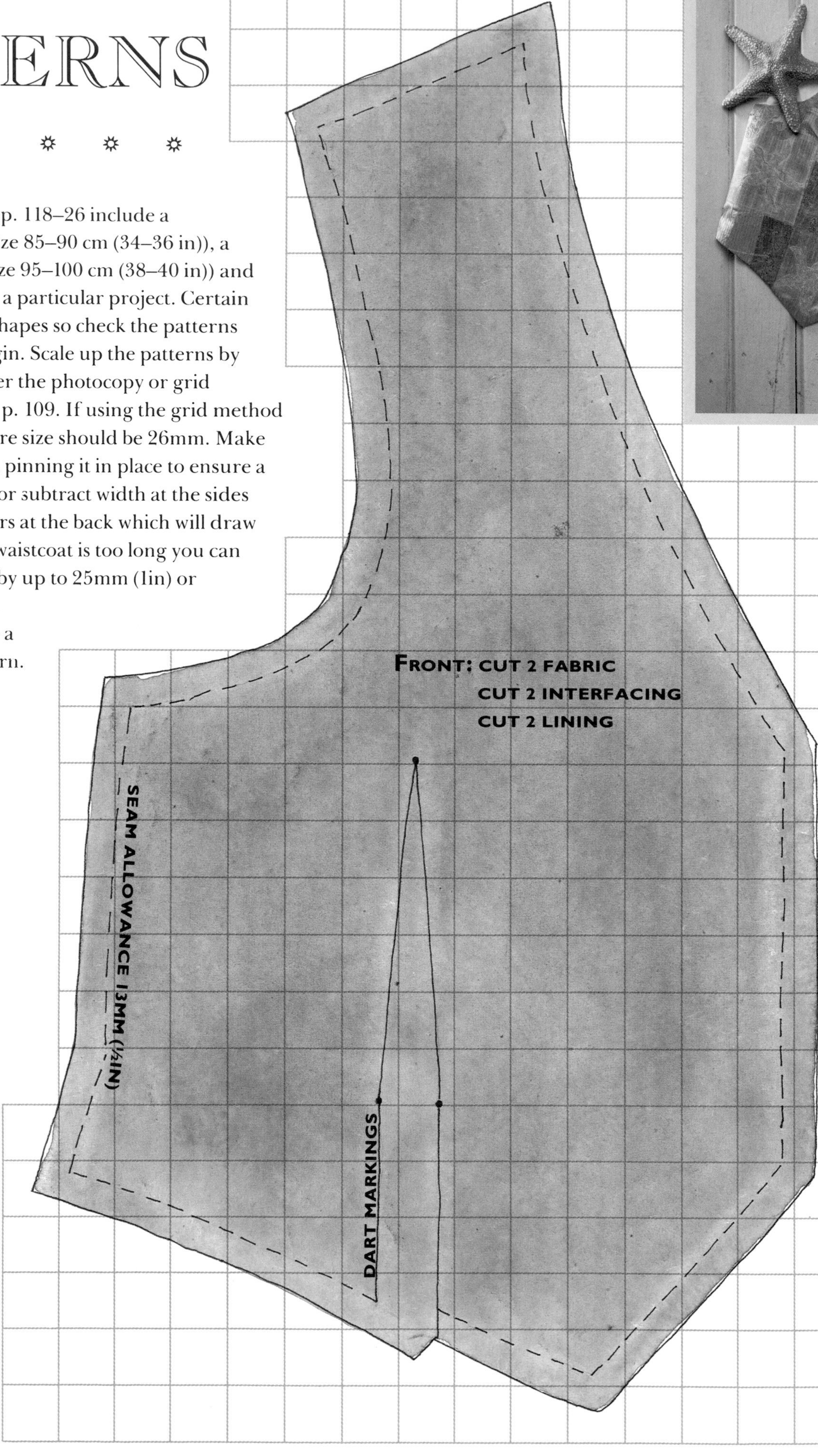

FRONT: CUT 2 FABRIC
CUT 2 INTERFACING
CUT 2 LINING

SEAM ALLOWANCE 13MM (½IN)

DART MARKINGS

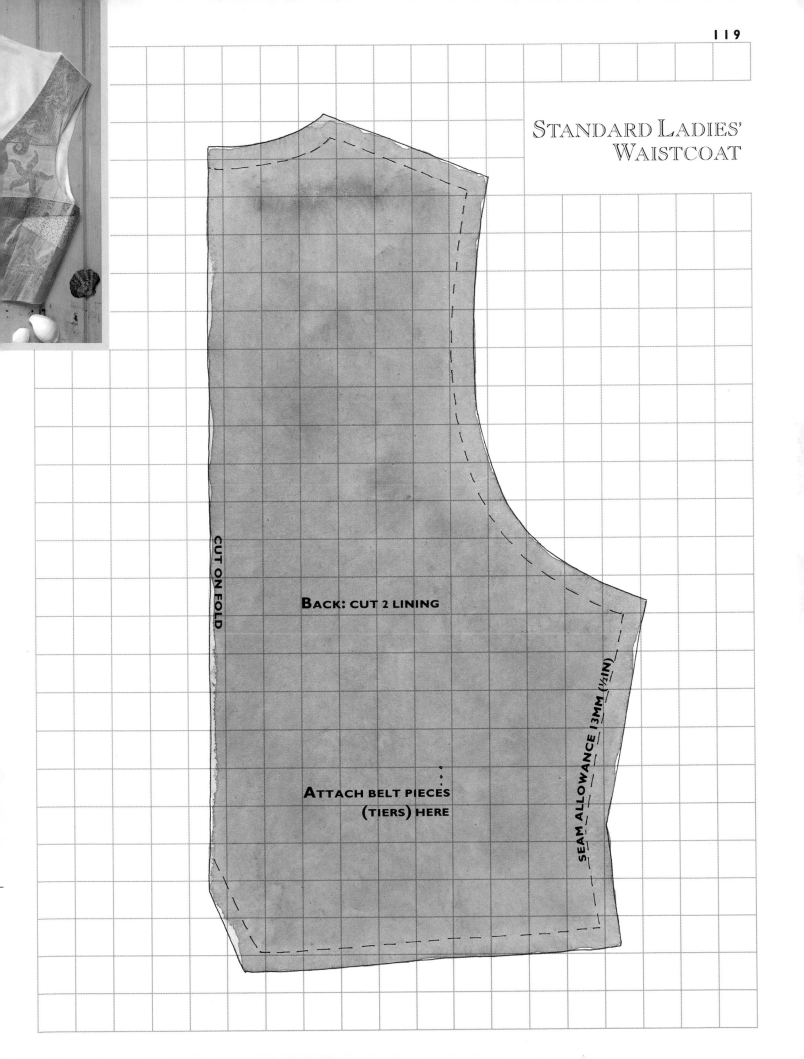

STANDARD LADIES'
WAISTCOAT

CUT ON FOLD

BACK: CUT 2 LINING

SEAM ALLOWANCE 13MM (½IN)

ATTACH BELT PIECES
(TIERS) HERE

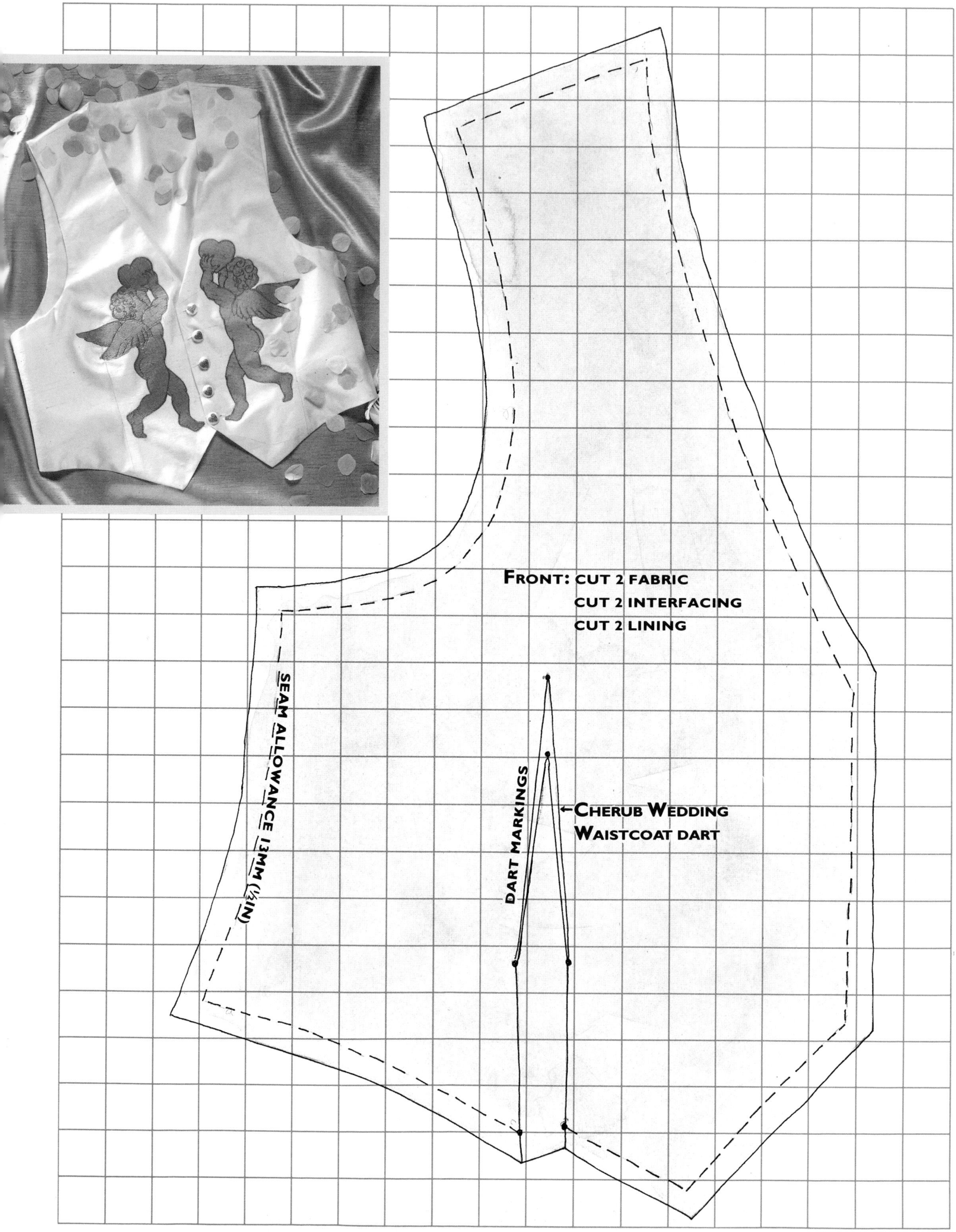

FRONT: CUT 2 FABRIC
CUT 2 INTERFACING
CUT 2 LINING

SEAM ALLOWANCE 13MM (½IN)

DART MARKINGS

←CHERUB WEDDING
WAISTCOAT DART

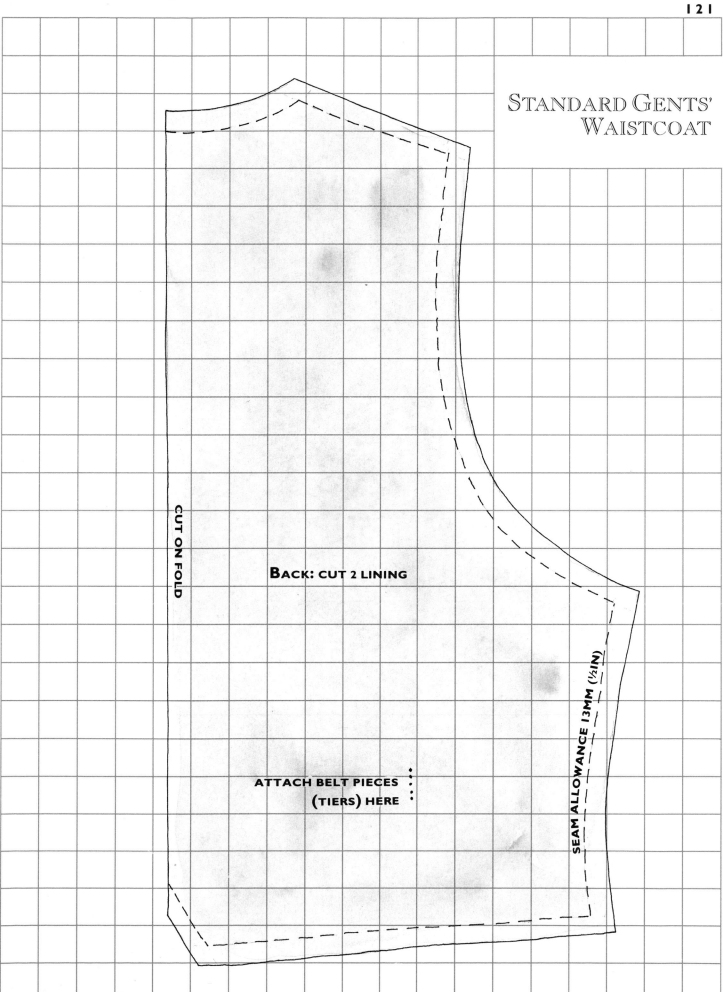

STANDARD GENTS'
WAISTCOAT

CUT ON FOLD

BACK: CUT 2 LINING

SEAM ALLOWANCE 13MM (½IN)

ATTACH BELT PIECES
(TIERS) HERE

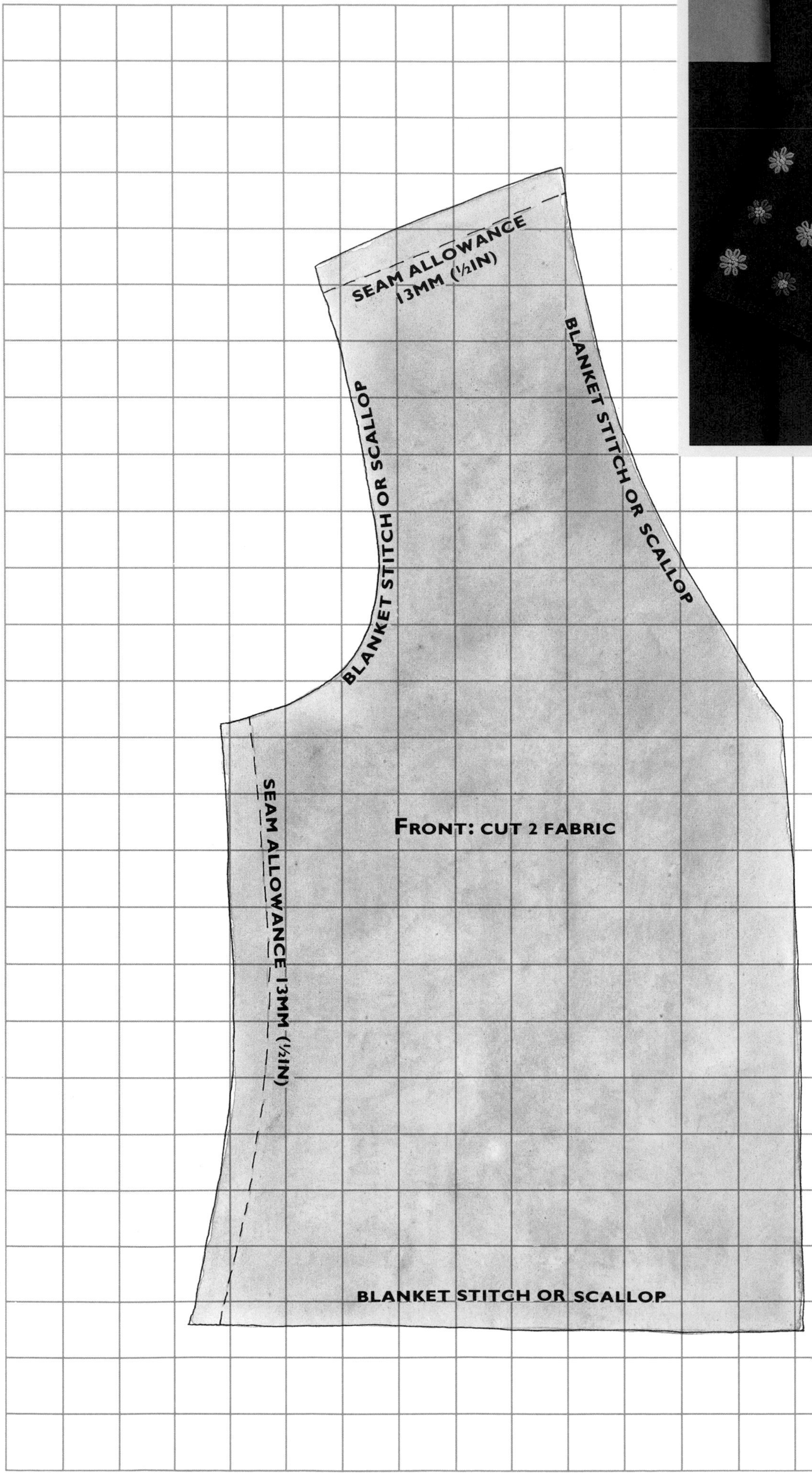

SEAM ALLOWANCE
13MM (½IN)

BLANKET STITCH OR SCALLOP

BLANKET STITCH OR SCALLOP

SEAM ALLOWANCE 13MM (½IN)

FRONT: CUT 2 FABRIC

BLANKET STITCH OR SCALLOP

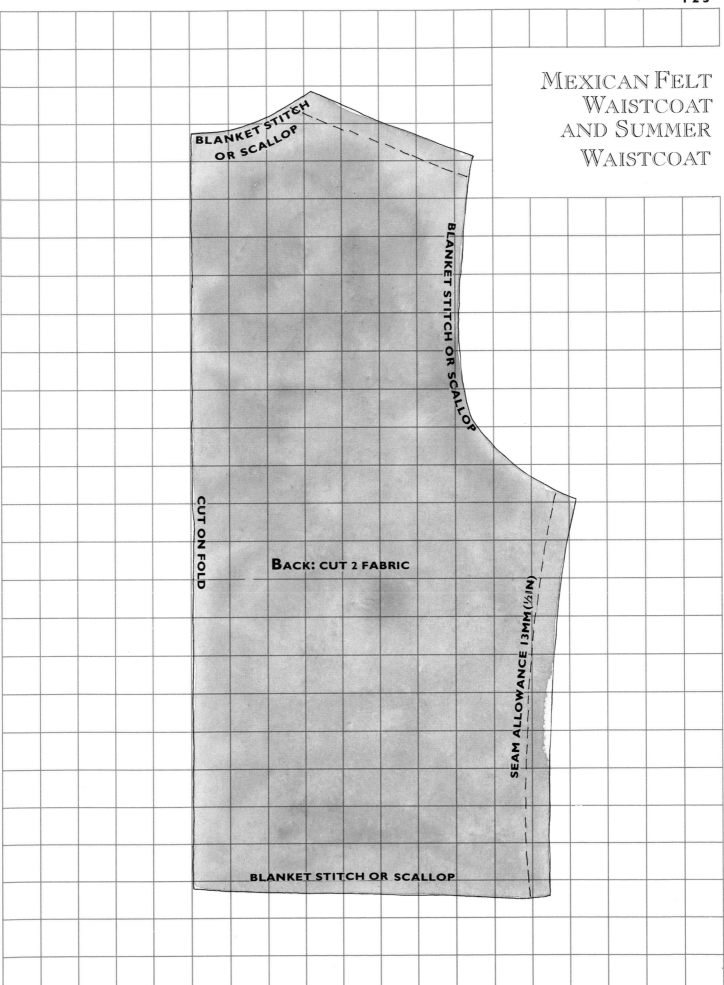

MEXICAN FELT
WAISTCOAT
AND SUMMER
WAISTCOAT

BLANKET STITCH
OR SCALLOP

BLANKET STITCH OR SCALLOP

CUT ON FOLD

BACK: CUT 2 FABRIC

SEAM ALLOWANCE 13MM (½IN)

BLANKET STITCH OR SCALLOP

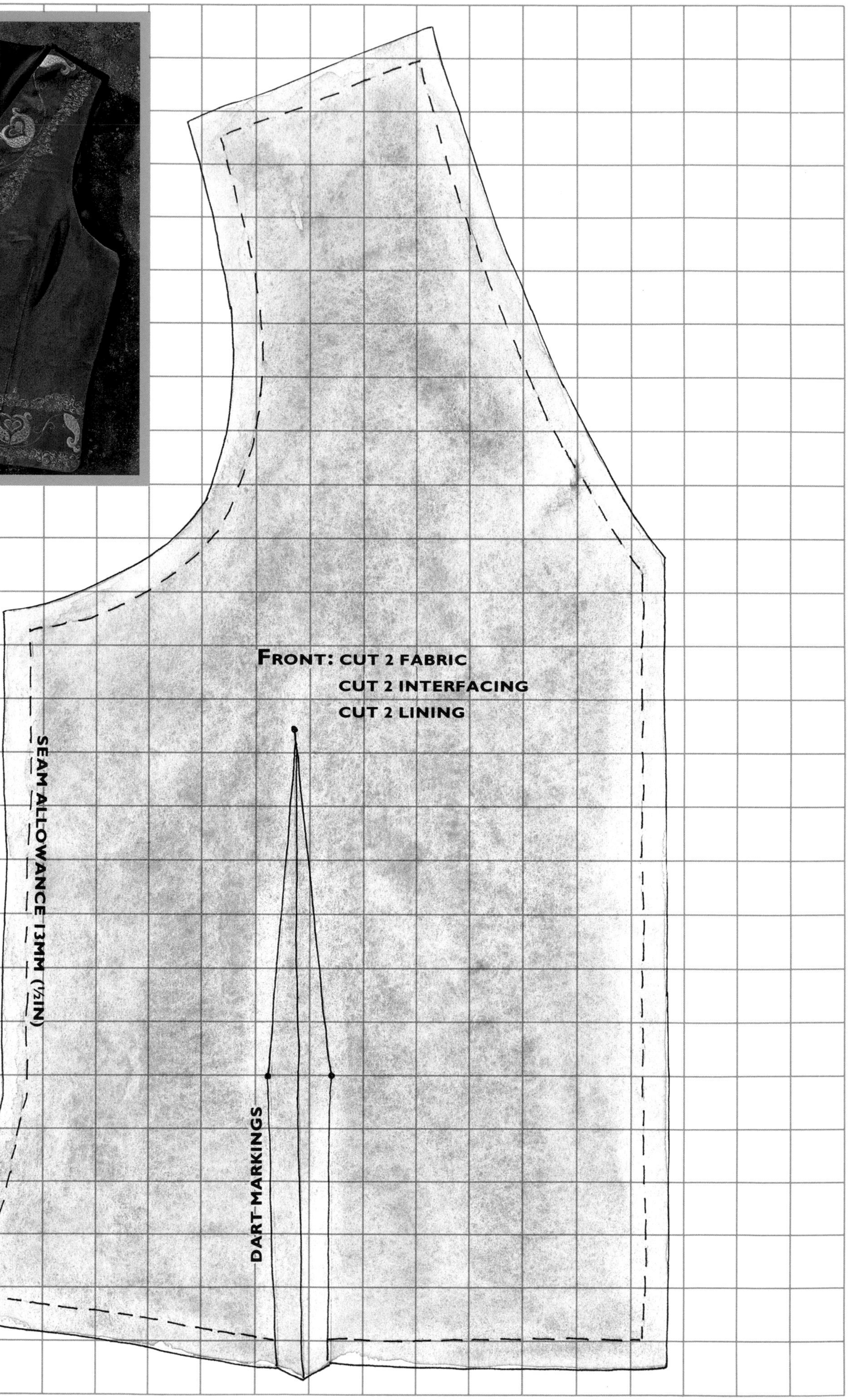

FRONT: CUT 2 FABRIC

CUT 2 INTERFACING

CUT 2 LINING

SEAM ALLOWANCE 13MM (½IN)

DART MARKINGS

VELVET FISH
WAISTCOAT

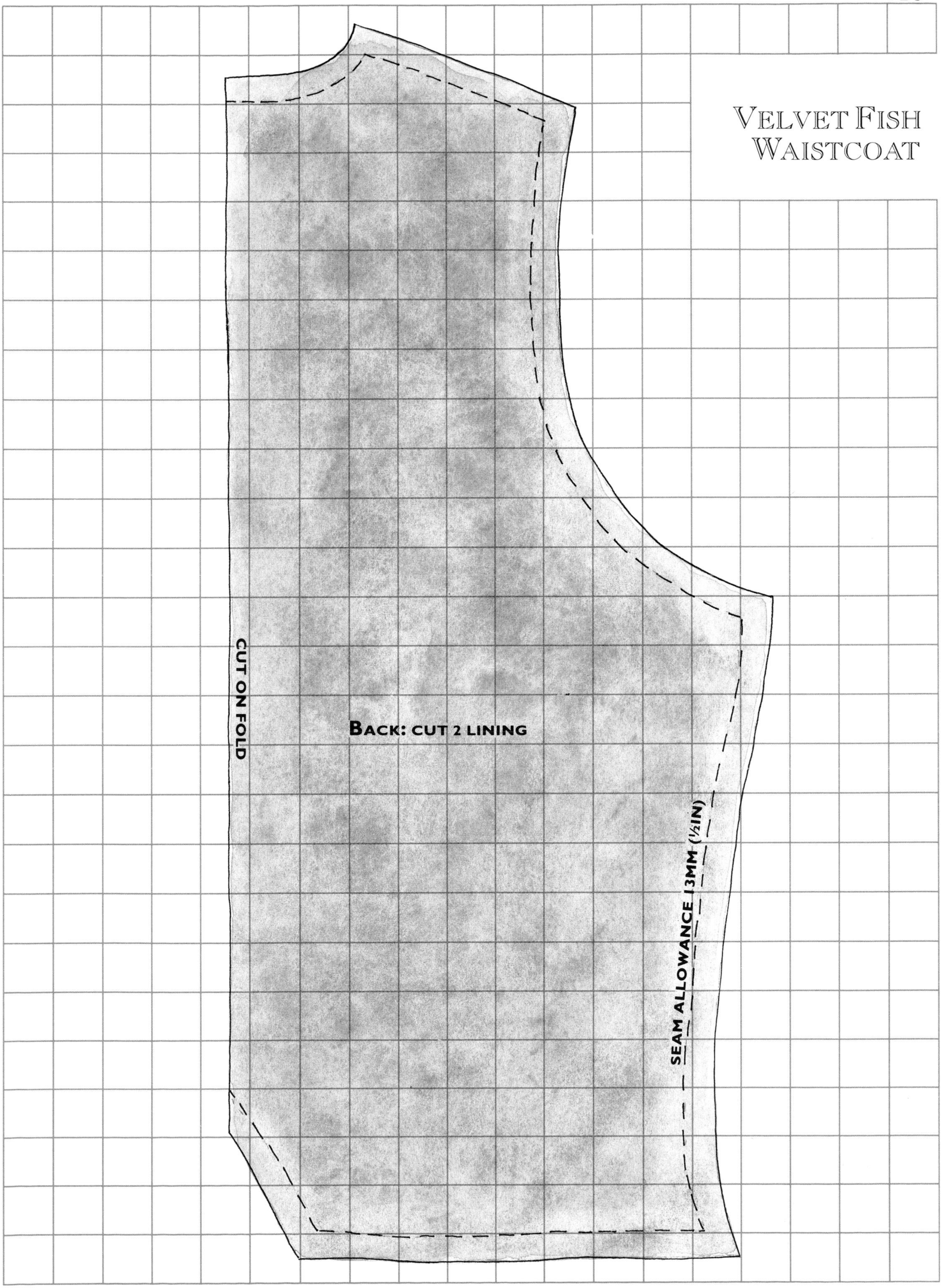

CUT ON FOLD

BACK: CUT 2 LINING

SEAM ALLOWANCE 13MM (½IN)

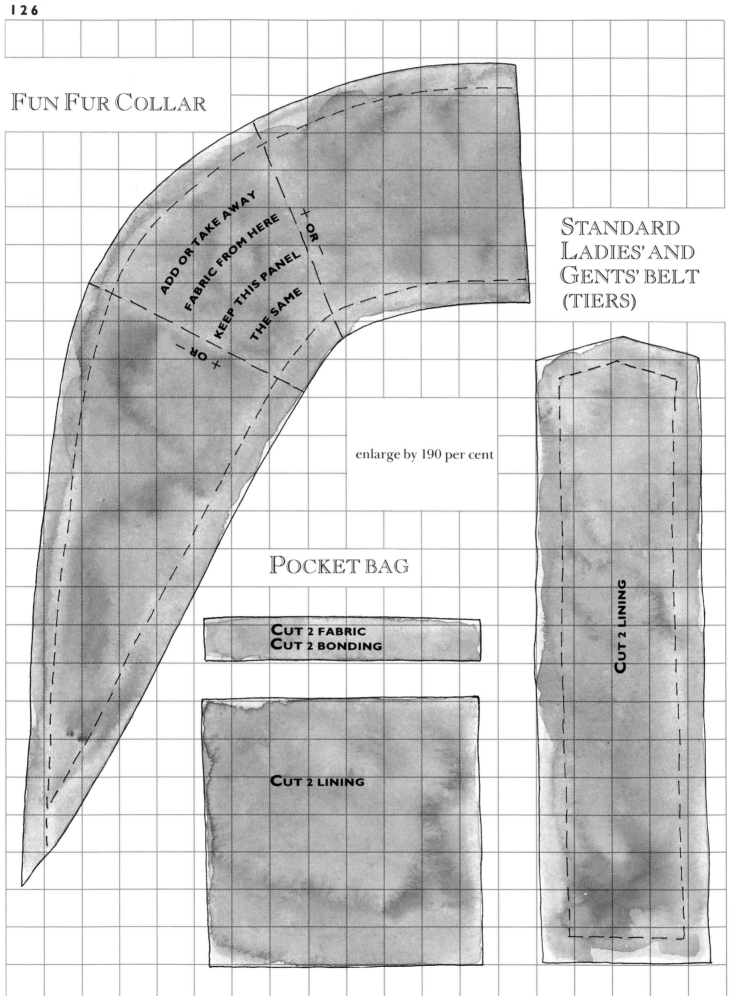

FUN FUR COLLAR

ADD OR TAKE AWAY
FABRIC FROM HERE
KEEP THIS PANEL
OR
THE SAME
OR

STANDARD LADIES' AND GENTS' BELT (TIERS)

enlarge by 190 per cent

CUT 2 LINING

POCKET BAG

CUT 2 FABRIC
CUT 2 BONDING

CUT 2 LINING

INDEX

CREDITS

The author would like to thank her parents and husband for their support. Also, thanks to Alistair McAuley, Carol Armour and Louise Brown for their special help.

Quarto Publishing would like to thank all the makers who contributed to the book:

Alison Bell, Arran Fine Art Silks, 4 Lakeside Place, Shiskine, Isle of Arran KA27 8EP
Pookie Blezard, Pazuki, 2 Beverley Gardens, London SW13 0LZ
Gilda Brown and **Shelagh O'Gorman,** 27 Flambard Rd, Harrow, Middlesex HA1 2NB
Toria Chaumeton, Torbagz Clothing Company, Unit 1.11b, Belgravia Workshops, 157–163 Marlborough Rd, London N19 4NF
Catherine Crowther, The Studio, Lovingtons, Great Yeldham, Halstead, Essex CO9 4HP
Sally Cunningham, 21 Solent Way, Alverstoke, Hampshire PO12 2NR
Jacqueline Farrell Textiles, The Old Church Studios, 92 Raeberry St, Glasgow G20 6EG
Judith Gait, St. Mary's Cottage, Hemington, Bath BA3 5XX
Gilbey's Waistcoat Gallery, 2 New Burlington Place, Savile Row, London W1
Deborah Gonet, 207b Chevening Rd, Queens Park, London NW6 6DT
Jo Hall, 6 Gilmore Drive, Prestwich, Manchester M25 5LB
Kate Haynes, 37 Parchment St, Winchester, Hants SO23 8BA
Caroline Keill, 86a Lorne Rd, London E7 0LL
Elspeth Kemp, 28 St Leonards Rd, Bangeo, Hertford, Herts SG14 3JW
Gaynor Kirby, Lesta Villa, Seaton Ross, York YO4 4LU
Rosemary MacCarthy Morrogh, 14 Marlborough Rd, Glenageary, Co. Dublin, Ireland
Liz McLean McKay, 24 Pauline Ave, Toronto, Canada/80 Fulwood Ave, Knightswood, Glasgow

Susie Moore, Waisted Art, 306 Hursley Rd, Chandlers Ford, Eastleigh, Hampshire SO5 1PF
Vera Morgan, 5 Penian, Deganwy, Llandudno, Gwynedd, North Wales LL30 1PE
Janet and Roger Quilter, Penpompren, Rhydcymerau, Nr. Landeilo, Dyfed SA19 7PP
Charles Robertson, 3 Syndenham Rd, Glasgow
Georgina von Etzdorf, 50 Burlington Arcade, London W1V 9AE

Quarto would also like to thank **Coats Crafts UK,** PO Box, McMullen Rd, Darlington, Co. Durham, DL1 1YQ for allowing us to use their pattern leaflet no. 4820 for the Sunflower Knit Waistcoat (pages 36–9) and for sponsorship of thread and fabric for the Rosebud Waistcoat (pages 64–7).

Index by Dorothy Frame